Professional Portfolios
A Collection of Articles

Edited by
Kay Burke

TRAINING AND PUBLISHING, INC.
Arlington Heights, Illinois

Professional Portfolios: A Collection of Articles

Published by IRI/SkyLight Training and Publishing, Inc.
2626 S. Clearbrook Dr., Arlington Heights, IL 60005
800-348-4474 or 847-290-6600
FAX 847-290-6609
info@iriskylight.com
http://www.iriskylight.com

Creative Director: Robin Fogarty
Managing Editor: Julia Noblitt
Editor: Sabine Vorkoeper
Proofreader: Edward Roberts
Researchers: Marilyn Foley, Amy Wolgemuth
Type Compositors: Donna Ramirez, Christina Georgi
Formatter: Donna Ramirez
Illustration and Cover Designer: David Stockman
Book Designers: Michael Melasi, Bruce Leckie
Production Supervisor: Bob Crump

ISBN 1-57517-013-2
LCCCN: 96-77237

1697B-4-97 V
Item number 1462
06 05 04 03 02 01 00 99 98 97   15 14 13 12 11 10 9 8 7 6 5 4 3 2

ontents

Professional Portfolios
A Collection of Articles

Although portfolios can be time-consuming to construct and cumbersome to review, they also can capture the complexities of professional practice in ways that no other approach can.—Kenneth Wolf

Please begin boarding the tour bus. Only one small suitcase per person is allowed. We will now embark on our annual 'Magical Mystery Staff Development Tour.' We'll be visiting four sites throughout the year, and our seven-hour tour packages require that you get off the bus at 8:30 and reboard again at 3:30 each day."

"This year's tour includes the following packages: Stop 1 in August—Strategic Planning; Stop 2 in October—Integrated Curricula; Stop 3 in February—Problem-Based Learning; and Stop 4 in April—Performance Assessment."

Sound familiar? In many staff development programs, just as on many European bus tours, everyone, regardless of their needs, prior knowledge, interests, or motivation, experiences the same thing. The programs are developed to comply with district goals, to meet state mandates, or to accommodate speaker availability. Too often teachers who do not have input into the decision-making process for what constitutes these staff development programs feel that the information they get is irrelevant to their own classes. Thus, they sometimes are unreceptive to the ideas presented in these one-day workshops. Others may welcome learning new ideas but feel that one "quick shot" of a topic du jour is not sufficient to understand the key concept or to implement ideas successfully. Comments like, "Our entire district has been trained in cooperative learning. We were 'inserviced' *one day* last August" are common. Rarely is a follow-up session scheduled or are attempts made to find out how many participants are actually applying what they have learned; rarely are participants provided with time to share what they are doing with peers. Moreover, these so-called "parachute drops" of staff development do not foster long-term transfer.

Structured bus tours, however, aren't always bad. Anyone who visits Europe for the first time (like most beginning teachers) usually appreciates the fact that there is a knowledgeable guide (staff developer) who speaks all the languages (educationese), who knows what places (hot topics) to visit, and who makes all the necessary arrangements (time, date, site, books). The tour provides security and routine since everything is new and since many aren't really sure where they want to go anyway. Some prefer to leave their travel plans to someone else because they're busy just trying to maintain their own classrooms (or, in the case of beginning teachers, just trying to establish teaching routines). Some have no idea where to go unless someone reviews the travel options with them.

The security of the "bus tour," however, turns to boredom after a few years, and veteran travelers begin to search for ways "to get off the bus." They yearn for the freedom of exploring on their own by strapping on a backpack and planning their own itinerary. Now that they've sampled the European tour, and have been exposed to all the options, they know which countries they want to return to, which ones they would rather avoid, and, most importantly, how long they want to spend in each country.

The analogy of the structure of the tour bus versus the freedom of the backpack journey describes the major difference between traditional staff development and a more focused and personalized staff development provided by a professional development portfolio. Traditional staff development, in many cases, calls for someone else to plan the itinerary; therefore, someone else has ownership of the journey. With a professional portfolio, on the other hand, the learners have ownership of their own travel plans. They determine their own needs and then utilize self-initiation, self-monitoring, and self-evaluation to reach their professional goals.

To continue the analogy of a journey, the travelers can use their backpack (or portfolio) to collect mementos or artifacts of the trip. They can also keep a travel log or journal to document their thoughts throughout the journey and take pictures and videos of memorable places, key events, or important people to include in the final album of the trip. Along the way, they can share their experiences with their peers and mentors, who provide meaningful and ongoing dialogue throughout the journey.

A professional portfolio, therefore, is very similar to an individualized backpack tour of Europe. The travelers make the decisions about what goals they would like to reach that year. For example, one teacher may want to experiment with using Gardner's theory of multiple intelligences in designing lessons and assessments. Another teacher may want to research how other educators are using portfolios in the classroom. Still another teacher may want to try using problem-based learning with science students.

Once educators have determined their goals and purposes for the year, they plan their itinerary by researching what has already been done in the field *before* beginning to explore new ideas on their own. Along the journey they collect products, documents, processes, and reflect on their findings. They continually discuss these findings with peers and mentors as they share the mementos their journey and anticipate their ETA (estimated time of arrival) for meeting their goal.

With the metaphor of the backpack journey in mind, the articles in this collection have been divided into three sections, each of which describes a different type of portfolio educators can develop to document their professional growth and development throughout their journey.

In section one, "Preservice Journey: The Academic Plan," college teachers discuss the various programs they have established to incorporate portfolios into their undergraduate or graduate programs. These programs require student teachers to document their progress in planning, classroom management, assessment, instruction, and communication in an ongoing portfolio. They also suggest that student teachers confer with others to discuss their learnings. In addition, the articles show that while some colleges assign grades for portfolios, others do not give traditional grades but include the portfolio component in their graduation requirements.

In section two, "Professional Development Journey: The Formative Plan," staff developers, administrators, and teachers discuss how teachers are designing their own Professional Development Plans (PDPs) at the beginning of each year by determining a focus for their work. Articles describe how they make these decisions on their own or after discussing ideas with peers, mentors, or supervisors, and how they subsequently document their progress throughout the year. The discussions illustrate how they share their findings with colleagues and/or supervisors at the end of each year. In addition, the collection suggests how these portfolios occasionally replace or supplement yearly observations. They are used primarily by educators to document their own progress in professional development—and not necessarily as evaluation tools.

The third section, "Performance Evaluation Journey: The Summative Plan," describes how some districts are asking educators to keep professional portfolios as part of their performance evaluation process. Authors discuss how these so-called high-stakes portfolios usually require standard criteria and some type of scoring method to help ensure validity and reliability, and how they are often evaluated by supervisors to assess a teacher's performance. Many authors stress "standards—but not standardization." They feel the portfolio provides the *framework* and sets the criteria, while teachers are free to include the items that show they are meeting their own goals.

In conclusion, professional portfolios can provide teacher/travelers with opportunities to plan their own professional development journey. They may not have the rigid structure of the "Staff Development Tour," which provides every staff member with the same professional development experience, but they do have a framework that invites teachers "to become architects of their own professional development by having them create portfolios based on individual growth plans" (Wolf 1996). This framework is essential or the portfolio might become "a scrapbook or steamer trunk . . . a collection of eye-catching and heart-warming mementoes that has strong personal meaning for the portfolio owner" (Wolf 1996).

Preparing a professional portfolio, therefore, represents an ongoing process of collecting and reflecting on artifacts and accomplishments over a specific time period as well as sharing concrete evidence and insights with mentors and colleagues on an ongoing basis. In the case of professional portfolios, the journey is just as important as the final destination.

"Attention all faculty. Pack your backpacks, plan your itineraries, and prepare to embark on your personalized tour of professional development." Let the journey begin!

Preservice Journey:
The Academic Plan

Assessment of development in teacher preparation programs is a challenge that does not lend itself readily to solution. Beyond assessment itself there is the further challenge of using the knowledge gained from assessment to reshape and improve programs. —Jo-Ann Snyder et al.

F aculty members in many colleges of education across the country are exploring more effective ways to assess the development of undergraduates in teacher preparation programs. They are struggling to create an evaluation system that does not rely solely on competency exit exams or clinical observations. Instead, they are trying to integrate several measurements that would not only certify their prospective teachers but also provide them with more specific feedback and encourage them to reflect on their own professional development. Many colleges of education, therefore, are experimenting with using professional portfolios in their teacher preparation programs.

The faculty members in the College of Education at Wayne State University in Detroit, Michigan, have developed a portfolio system as a program requirement for prospective teachers, as described in "Beyond Assessment: University/School Collaboration in Portfolio Review and the Challenge to Program Improvement" by Jo-Ann Snyder et al. The faculty selected ten competencies the students had to demonstrate through the selection of artifacts for their portfolios. At the end of the program, two-person teams made up of principals, teachers, curriculum leaders, counselors, superintendents, and university faculty held thirty-minute portfolio conferences with the students. The feedback from the program has been very positive, and the faculty is now revising the process to make it more effective.

In the article "The Portfolio: Sonnet, Mirror and Map," Mary Diez describes three ways that the portfolio process helps education majors at Alverno College in Milwaukee, Wisconsin. She uses the metaphor of the *sonnet,* the *mirror,* and the *map* to identify three phases of portfolio development. According to Diez, a sonnet, like a portfolio, provides a framework for the process, but the contents of the portfolio, like the poetic words of a sonnet, can showcase creativity and diversity. The mirror metaphor captures the reflective nature of a developmental portfolio as it allows students to "see themselves" over time. The last metaphor, that of the map, symbolizes creating a plan and setting goals. After reviewing the evidence collected over time, prospective teachers can reflect on where they were, where they are now, and, most importantly, where they want to go. Throughout this process of collection, reflection, and self-assessment, students are learning about themselves as well as beginning their journey of professional development.

Lucindia Chance and Thomas Rakes, in the article entitled "Differentiated Evaluation in Professional Development Schools: An Alternative Paradigm for Preservice Teacher Evaluation," describe how student teachers in the College of Education at the University of Memphis engage in a comprehensive evaluation program that requires creation of a portfolio containing essential demographic data *as well as* using a five-point scale to evaluate planning, communication, leadership, teaching strategies, classroom management, and evaluation. The evaluation program also requires student teachers to submit unit lesson plans, sample lessons, student work samples, and daily logs. In addition, supervisors conduct nine five-minute "snapshot" visits and fill out observation checklists. The collaboration process among student teachers, supervising teachers, and college supervisors encourages not only a more comprehensive evaluation of student teachers, but also helps the student teachers become more reflective practitioners. According to Chance and Rakes, "The use of a portfolio system is a part of an overall belief that authentic assessment should be a part of the overall student teaching process."

Based on a review of the three college programs described in the articles that follow, as well as a review of the literature, students in preservice programs in which portfolios are required usually:

1. know the purposes of their portfolio;
2. follow prescribed guidelines but are allowed to make choices about what they want to include;
3. know the criteria by which they will be evaluated;
4. select evidence that meets goals, criteria, or competencies;
5. discuss their work with peers and supervisors regularly;
6. integrate theory into practice;
7. share their final portfolio with a wider audience and receive written and oral feedback and/or a grade; and
8. find the portfolio process to be helpful in their teaching and for future professional growth.

The use of portfolios in preservice programs is increasing dramatically. But as Diez states,

> The challenge for all of us engaged in the design of portfolio assessment is to assist our students to learn how to make their products more "interwoven and complete," weighing "the stress of every chord" to assure that the portfolio becomes an expression worthy of their—and our—time and effort.

Beyond Assessment: University/School Collaboration in Portfolio Review and the Challenge to Program Improvement

by Jo-Ann Snyder, Sharon Elliott, Navaz Peshotan Bhavnagri, and James Boyer

Assessment of development in teacher preparation programs is a challenge that does not lend itself readily to solution. Beyond assessment itself, there is the further challenge of using the knowledge gained from assessment to reshape and improve programs. The common practice of assigning trained professionals to observe students in clinical settings and share observations and assessments with them over an extended period of time is still perhaps the best method available to teacher educators who must assess performance that is not adequately measured by traditional question and answer tests. But even where this approach functions best, it is generally carried out on a personal level, which can be of great benefit to the developing student but offers less likelihood that knowledge gained by professionals in the process will find its way into any systematic process for program improvement. In order to create a way to provide feedback to its teacher preparation program, the College of Education at Wayne State University began to explore the use of portfolios in the program. The College saw the potential of the portfolio process for informing the program as well as the students in the program.

From *Action in Teacher Education*, vol. 15, no. 4, Winter 1993–1994, pp. 55–60. © 1993 by the Association of Teacher Educators. Reprinted with permission.

The Ohio Consortium for Portfolio Development (Central State University, University of Dayton, Wright State University and the Dayton Public Schools) has worked for several years on the use of portfolios to document students' growth, knowledge of content and development of reflective abilities (Cole, 1991, 1992). The Consortium recognized that portfolios are both a process and a product.

From the outset, Wayne State Faculty viewed the portfolio process as a self-assessment tool.

It is as a process that portfolios can be significant in developing reflection among teacher education students and teachers. When students and teachers make decisions about the way in which they organize portfolios, they need to reflect about their understanding of professional roles and responsibilities (Cole, et al. 1991, p. 4).

From the outset, Wayne State faculty viewed the portfolio process as a self-assessment tool to be used in a University/ School partnership that would cut across academic disciplines, roles and responsibilities. Using the portfolio to strengthen this collaboration sets this approach apart from other assessments used in teacher evaluation programs (Collins, 1990; Terry, Backman & Eade, 1983). Throughout this process, faculty are also pushed to reflect on their roles as teacher educators and on the effectiveness of program elements, including course offerings, field experiences and program directions. Students are challenged to reflect upon their experiences in the program as they move toward becoming teachers.

Wayne State is an urban University with an enrollment of approximately 34,000 students. The College of Education enrolls approximately 3,500 students, a third of whom are in initial teacher preparation programs. The University is located virtually in the geographic center of the City of Detroit and draws its student population primarily from six counties in southeast Michigan. In preparation for the NCATE internal review process, the College of Education in 1991 adopted as an organizing theme "The Urban Educator as a Reflective Innovative Professional" (1990). The faculty felt that this theme, in the words of Galluzzo and Pankratz, "captures the consensus of faculty beliefs and describes the type of teacher the program seeks to graduate" (p. 10).

Using the theme as a starting point, the Teacher Education faculty developed ten teaching competencies that students would be required to demonstrate through the development and presentation of portfolios.

CONTENTS OF PORTFOLIOS

It was decided that the portfolio process would provide concrete evidence that students have developed in the following ten areas:

1. knows academic content and a variety of teaching methods;
2. organizes and implements effective instructional programs;
3. demonstrates appropriate classroom management techniques to ensure a safe and orderly environment conducive to learning;
4. stimulates creative and critical thinking;
5. has knowledge of human growth and development;
6. has a commitment to students and their learning;
7. uses listening, speaking, reading and writing skills effectively;
8. behaves in an ethical, reflective and professional manner;
9. understands the importance of multicultural perspectives; and
10. applies appropriate assessment, evaluation and testing procedures

IMPLEMENTATION OF THE PROJECT

Students in the WSU teacher certification program have from two to four semesters of pre-student teaching and student teaching experiences in K–12 schools. Elementary education students have two semesters of pre-student teaching (four half days a week) and one semester of student teaching (five full days). Secondary education students have one semester of pre-student teaching (five half days a week) and one semester of student teaching (five full days a week). Early childhood, special education and bilingual education students have two semesters of pre-student teaching and two semesters of student teaching.

In the Fall of 1991 the portfolio process was introduced as an option to Elementary Education instructors who teach methods courses and supervise the first pre-student teaching experience. Several instructors chose to participate in this pilot process involving approximately 75 students who began developing their portfolios that term. In the Winter term, 1992, portfolios became a requirement for all students in their first pre-student teaching experience, involving approximately 250 students. In the Fall of 1992 the portfolio was made a requirement for all students in certification programs and no student could receive a grade for student teaching without developing and presenting a portfolio. This gradual implementation provided a full academic year to educate students regarding the process and the product, and to make the faculty a part of the process. By Winter, 1993, all 1000 certification students were involved in portfolio development.

> In the Winter term, 1992, portfolios became a requirement for all students in their first pre-student teaching experience.

ORIENTATION

Staff and students were given printed material stating the purpose of the project, listing expectations and outlining a possible format for the portfolio. They were also given copies of recent articles on the use of portfolios and were provided with opportunities to discuss the project and brainstorm ideas with project directors.

A series of student workshops, required and optional, were conducted to explain the purpose of the portfolio assignment and give concrete suggestions for selecting and organizing content. Students were also given printed material suggesting the following format for presentations:

• a brief introduction including name, teaching major and minor and other such pertinent information,

• a summary of field experiences, pre-student teaching and student teaching,

• a short review of materials included in the portfolio, and

• a ten to fifteen minute expansion on the highlights of the portfolio.

Students were informed that portfolios would not be graded, but that development and presentation of a portfolio would be required to receive a grade for student teaching. Once the portfolio became a requirement for program completion, faculty and students alike began displaying a serious level of involvement and commitment to the process. In December, 1992, 236 portfolios were presented. Only four students completing student teaching failed to meet the requirement, choosing instead to have their grades deferred to a later time.

PORTFOLIO REVIEW

One hundred fifty letters were sent to principals, teachers, curriculum leaders, counselors, superintendents, university faculty, administrators and Education alumni inviting them to participate as reviewers in the portfolio process. A total of 100 people agreed to participate. Twelve school districts were represented, one of which was the Detroit Public School System which had twenty-four different schools represented. Fifteen faculty from the Teacher Education Division served as reviewers along with faculty from other units in the College and the University. The Dean and all assistant deans in the College of Education also served as reviewers.

> **Each two person team reviewed between three and five portfolios in half hour blocks of time.**

Reviewers were assigned to two person teams and given a choice of reviewing in a four hour block of time during an evening or on a Saturday. Professions from the schools were teamed with University personnel in an attempt to broaden the perspectives of the reviewing teams. Each two person team reviewed between three and five portfolios in half hour blocks of time. Students were assigned on the basis of their time preferences. No attempt was made to match academic specializations of students and reviewers. The anticipation was that the invited reviewers would be fully capable of assessing levels of professional knowledge and teaching skills regardless of academic specialties.

Reviewers were asked to arrive one half hour before the presentations began to provide time for refreshments, a short orientation and an opportunity to meet and visit with other reviewers assigned to the same block of time. The reviewers had five to ten minutes to ask questions for clarification or offer suggestions which might expand or improve the portfolio. At the end of the presentations, reviewers and students were given reaction sheets to record their assessments of the overall process as well as of the individual presentations.

STUDENT RESPONSES

Students were asked four questions regarding the portfolio process. With each question there was an opportunity to make additional comments: (1) Do you think the portfolio represented you favorably as a beginning professional?; (2) Do you feel you were given enough time to develop your portfolio?; (3) On a scale of one to five with five being high, how would you rate the help you received from cooperating teachers, WSU instructors and field supervisors in developing your portfolio?; and (4) What suggestions would you make to improve the portfolio process?

> Most [students] felt that the portfolio presented an accurate picture of their skills and experiences.

Two hundred thirty of the 236 students completed the student response sheet. In response to the first question relative to how well the presentation represented the student's professional skills, 88% of the students answered yes. Most [students] felt that the portfolio presented an accurate picture of their skills and experiences. A typical comment was, "The portfolio is a good way to give a brief synopsis of the work I have done to prepare myself for becoming a teacher." Students also commented that the portfolio helped them clarify exactly what they had done in their pre-student teaching and student teaching assignments and had given them a chance to articulate some of their beliefs regarding education. They also saw the advantage of recognizing areas that needed improvement. A number of students commented that they had begun to see themselves as teachers rather than University students. Of the 12% who felt the portfolios did not reflect their skills as teachers, the most prevalent comment was that they found it difficult to present some of the intangibles of classroom teaching in the portfolio format. One comment referred to the difficulty of documenting the teacher's "manner" with children; another referred to the difficulty of "describing yourself on paper."

In response to the second question, students did not feel that they had enough time to prepare the portfolios; some stated that they felt "rushed," especially during this time when they were trying to devote their full attention to student teaching. This was the reason given by the four students who elected to defer their student teaching grades and present their portfolios after completing the student teaching experience. Others stated that they were unsure of the expectations of the assignment. One student summed up her difficulty with the assignment by stating, "I feel it's hard to put into words who I am in so few pages."

Virtually all of the students stated that they were glad the portfolio requirement had been implemented.

In response to the third question asking students to rate the help they received from professionals in preparing their portfolios, responses were distributed as follows:

Excellent	5	20%
	4	10%
Fair	3	21%
	2	27%
Poor	1	20%
No Answer		2%

This distribution may reflect the large number of students completing the assignment and the varying ways that instructors and supervisors interpreted the requirement to their students.

The fourth question asked for suggestions for improving the process of portfolio development and review. Most responses clustered around two concerns: "better directions" and "more time to complete the assignment." Other suggestions were: students be given examples and sample portfolios; uniform content be required; and the format be made open because of the opportunity that would provide for creative ideas. Virtually all of the students stated that they were glad the portfolio requirement had been implemented. The element for which they expressed most appreciation was the feedback from reviewers. They overwhelmingly agreed with the decision not to assign a grade for the portfolio.

REVIEWER RESPONSES

Reviewers were asked six questions: (1) Do you think the portfolios adequately represented the students as beginning professionals?; (2) Do you feel the students were given enough time to present their portfolios and receive responses from reviewers?; (3) Did the presentations further your understanding of the Teacher Education program at Wayne State?; (4) What is your overall impression of Wayne State University students as a group?; (5) Why did you agree to serve as a reviewer?; and (6) What suggestions would you make to improve the portfolio process?

Of the 90 reviewers who completed the response forms, 98% reported that the portfolios represented the students favorably as beginning teachers. Perhaps more significant than the percentage of positive responses were the comments made by reviewers relative to the portfolios as representations of beginning professions. Typical comments were: "a fairly accurate picture of the students—much better than expected"; "a good medium for dialogue and interchange of ideas"; and "creative."

Some comments focused on the purposes that could be served by this activity: "The presentations provide students with the opportunity to present the best of their experiences as beginning educators"; and "This concept is an excellent one. It certainly will help students develop confidence...."

In response to the third question asking if the reviewers' understanding of the teacher preparation program was furthered by the presentation, 94% said "Yes." The remaining 6% who said "No" were all Teacher Education faculty who were already familiar with the program. Almost half the respondents identified specific elements of the teacher preparation program for which they gained appreciation as a result of their involvement in the review process. Most frequently mentioned were: (1) emphasis of the program on multi-cultural education; (2) focus on integration of urban and suburban issues; (3) interdisciplinary nature of the teacher preparation program; and (4) the varied field experiences of the student teaching program. One reviewer commented,

> It was great to see what is going on in other disciplines. The process reinforces the notion of cross disciplinary education. We can't isolate ourselves. If teachers learn to work and support each other's subject matter, hopefully students can see many types of relationships.

Three reviewers who were teacher education faculty stated that the reviewing process enhanced their own professional development. Typical comments were: "It gave me ideas for improving my methods classes"; "helped me to see how to refine our students' idea of the portfolio"; and "what was particularly helpful for me is that I now have a better understanding of how I can help prepare my students for this process!"

Three reviewers stated that the reviewing process enhanced their own professional development.

Reviewers gave a wide range of responses to the question of why they agreed to participate in the process. Reasons given included: "commitment to portfolios as a tool for assessment"; "commitment to the University's efforts in teacher preparation"; "desire to learn how the program was attempting to develop reflective educators"; "reciprocation to the College for placing student teachers in their schools"; and "it sounded like it would be enjoyable and interesting." Teacher Education faculty stated that they felt a commitment to help their students in their preparation as future professionals.

The list of suggestions given by reviewers for improving the process gave a clear indication that reviewers took the experience seriously. Some observed that students had varying degrees of understanding regarding content and format of the portfolio and needed more specific direction for organizing and preparing for the presentation. Other suggestions focused on the portfolio being used for interviews. They suggested that students be given guidance on how to present portfolios at job interviews and that a library of exemplary portfolios be developed and seminars offered where students can share, discuss, and review each other's portfolios. There were other suggestions that students be included on the review panels.

FINDINGS AND CONCLUSIONS

To a great extent, the first objective of the project, to provide concrete evidence that students have satisfactorily developed competence in ten specific areas, was met. Although not always specifically labeled, the activities or lessons chosen by the students to be included in portfolios consistently reflected seven of the ten competencies and were recognized as such by the reviewers, as witnessed by such comments as "understands multicultural perspectives," and "knows content and methods of teaching." Three skill areas that did not emerge prominently in this process were: "demonstrates appropriate classroom management techniques to ensure a safe and orderly environment conducive to learning"; "has knowledge of human growth and development"; and "applies appropriate assessment, evaluation and testing procedures." This may have been the result of too little guidance in the preparation of the portfolios or the lack of emphasis on these areas in the program. This first attempt at requiring all students completing the program to develop a portfolio has set the stage for developing a valuable assessment tool to be used by the Teacher Education faculty.

> The most surprising outcome in this first round was the level of enthusiasm displayed.

Probably the most surprising outcome in this first round was the level of enthusiasm displayed throughout the process by school personnel and faculty from throughout the university. The half-hour orientation for reviewers turned out to be an excellent device for quickly immersing reviewers in the process. Many saw it as an opportunity for a personal and professional exchange of ideas and took full advantage of the situation. Spirited discussions in these sessions far exceeded expectations and were extremely encouraging from the perspective of university/school relations.

Project directors, in assisting students and faculty in the portfolio development process, observing the review process, and evaluating the response sheets, were made aware that there were omissions in the competencies listed. One omission was "skill in working with parents and support staff." Other objectives were not worded as well as they might have been in materials distributed to students and faculty. A positive result is that the faculty has decided to review all competencies required in the certification program.

The objectives of enhancing collaboration among university and school personnel, renewing commitment throughout the University, and increasing knowledge regarding the teacher preparation program were achieved to a far greater extent than originally anticipated. Faculty members, college and university administrators and school personnel were extremely enthusiastic in their participation and responses to the questionnaires. Virtually all expressed a desire to help new professionals and emphasized how much they enjoyed the experience. All but one said they would serve again if invited. A strong sense of collegiality emerged during the review process that will be built upon in future efforts.

> Changes in requirements and procedures are being made in preparation for the next round.

The College learned a great deal from this round of portfolio development and presentation, and changes in requirements and procedures are being made in preparation for the next round. Beginning with pre-student teaching, students will have opportunities for continued dialogue, seminars and forums for exchange of ideas on portfolio development. These exchanges will allow for feedback prior to the final presentation. At a monthly student teaching seminar, former students who have presented outstanding portfolios the previous term will share their thoughts about the process. There will also be greater emphasis in pre-student teaching coursework on the reflective decisions students are expected to make, as well as on the guidance they need as they develop their portfolios. Student responses to this first large-scale experience with portfolios [have] served to intensify faculty commitment to continue and improve the process. Many reported that they took reviewers' comments and suggestions very seriously and that they came away from the process with a feeling of elation.

In future rounds the purpose of the portfolio must be made clearer to reviewers. Printed materials given to reviewers will be the same as that given to faculty and students; however, it will probably have to be expanded to accommodate first time reviewers who will need more background information than students and faculty involved in the program on a daily basis. Orientation sessions for reviewers will continue, but will focus more on the need to assess presentations on the basis of the stated objectives. Reviewers and students must have a common perception of the purpose of the portfolio: it is not a product for presentation at a job interview, even though that may be a logical next step. The purpose, from the College perspective, is to assist students in fine tuning their teaching skills, and to guide faculty in the on-going process of program improvement. Based on the results of this effort, the portfolio process not only appears well suited to the goals of student and program evaluation, but goes beyond this assessment and builds collaboration with schools. The College of Education at Wayne State is committed to making it a permanent part of the teacher preparation program.

REFERENCES

Cole, D. J. (1992, February). *The developing professional: Process and product portfolios.* Paper presented at the Annual Meeting of the American Association of Colleges for Teacher Education in San Antonio, Texas. (ERIC Document Reproduction Service No. ED 342 731)

Cole, D. J., Messner, P. E., Swonigan, H., & Tillman, B. (1991). *Portfolio structure and student profiles: An analysis of education student portfolio reflectivity.* Paper presented at the Annual Meeting of the American Education Research Association in Chicago, Illinois. (ERIC Document Reproductive Service No. ED 335 307)

Collins, A. (1990). *Novices, experts, veterans, and masters: The role of content and pedagogical knowledge in evaluating teaching.* NY: Carnegie Corp. of NY. (ERIC Document Reproduction Service No. ED 319 815)

Galluzzo, G., & Pankratz, R. S. (1990). Five attributes of a teacher education program knowledge base. *Journal of Teacher Education, 41*(4), 7–14.

Terry, G. L., Backman, C. A., & Eade, G. E. (1983). *The portfolio process in professional development.* Pensacola, FL: The University of West Florida. (ERIC Document Reproduction Service No. ED 227 073)

The Portfolio: Sonnet, Mirror and Map

by Mary E. Diez

The portfolio offers encouragement for reflection in at least three ways. First, it provides both the discipline and the freedom of structure, allowing one to see one's own work. Second, it provides the opportunity to assess one's own strengths and weaknesses through examination of a collection of samples, as well as to get feedback on one's performance from others. Third, the process of self-assessment leads one to setting goals for future development and professional growth.

I am pleased to be part of the University of Redlands and Rockefeller Brothers Fund Conference *Linking Liberal Arts and Teacher Education: Encouraging Reflection through Portfolios.* The tradition of liberal arts teacher education in the United States has many strengths; important among them is the practice of examining one's own practice and reflecting on one's own growth. I come to this talk as well with a special interest in the liberal arts, having served as a faculty member in English and communication before moving into the role of teacher educator.

As suggested by the title, this reflection on the use of portfolios will be divided into three parts, three angles for looking at the theme of encouraging reflection through portfolios: the sonnet, the mirror and the map.

PORTFOLIO AS SONNET

Why choose the image of the sonnet for portfolio assessment? I'm sure most of us have at least a passing acquaintance with the

Paper presented at the Conference on Linking Liberal Arts and Teacher Education: Encouraging Reflection through Portfolios, San Diego, California, October 6, 1994, ED 378 148. © 1994 by Mary E. Diez. Reprinted with permission.

form of the sonnet—14 lines of iambic pentameter, with variations of rhyme schemes and thought construction (the Petrarchan/Italian and the Elizabethan/Shakespearean are the two most common types). But what does the sonnet have to do with portfolios?

I think the following sonnet about sonnets from William Wordsworth provides a clue. "Nuns Fret Not" is a poem I have used in an interdisciplinary course where students engaged in exploration of the relationships between form and meaning.

Nuns Fret Not
Nuns fret not at their convent's narrow room;
And hermits are contented with their cells;
And students with their pensive citadels;
Maids at the wheel, the weaver at his loom,
Sit blithe and happy; bees that soar for bloom,
High as the highest Peak of Furness-fells,
Will murmur by the hour in foxglove bells:
In truth the prison, unto which we doom
Ourselves, no prison is: and hence for me,
In sundry moods, 'twas pastime to be bound
Within the sonnet's scanty plot of ground;
Pleased if some souls (for such there needs must be)
Who have felt the weight of too much liberty,
Should find brief solace there, as I have found.
                    —William Wordsworth 1807

Wordsworth was one of several poets who used the medium of the sonnet to explore whether the sonnet (and by extension any particular form of poetry) was too rigid. His answer: *what constrains also frees.* The first part of the poem gathers examples of where an apparent limit is seen as providing benefit. Thus, the limits of the sonnet's "scanty plot of ground" challenge the poet to capture his or her idea in a specific shape. When it "works," the meaning and form together create exquisite beauty. Wordsworth does not address directly another question: Does following the form of the sonnet make a good poem? I'm sure he would not argue that the form, in itself, assures a beautiful expression. Rather, the form provides a structure for the meaning to be expressed. And this is the point of my first analogy: the portfolio as sonnet.

The portfolio, like the sonnet, is simply a form, a structure. Provided one puts quality work between its covers, the portfolio can be a structure to help an individual express meaning. But its quality depends [upon] what the individual does with it. Too often I hear teachers fall into the trap of expecting the *form* to do the work that only human discipline and creativity can do. I recall hearing one of the teachers in a summer workshop on portfolio assessment say to her group, "What if *it* doesn't work?" Portfolio assessment is not an *it*, with independent power. *We* have to make it work. The portfolio may provide a form, but the agency remains with the teacher's and student's *use* of the form. My argument is that form, whether for a poem or a portfolio, can be seen as a discipline that can be used to shape expression. It does not do the work of expression—that's the poet['s] and the student's role.

In the showcase portfolio, one's performance is focused outward, toward other persons.

The type of portfolio that the sonnet metaphor best describes is the *showcase* portfolio. A showcase portfolio puts together samples of one's work, with the purpose of, for example, showing the range of performance one has demonstrated, showing examples that meet a set of criteria for performance, or showing samples that one considers one's best efforts. It is usually created for a particular audience and purpose, as when an artist puts together a collection of samples to be considered for inclusion in a gallery exhibition. In the showcase portfolio, one's performance is focused outward, toward other persons, in the same way that literary works are written with a sense of the audience who will read them.

This external focus is one of the reasons why discipline is an issue with the showcase portfolio. In literature—whether sonnet or short story—all the parts must work together and have a relationship to the meaning that the author intends to be communicated to the reader. In the work world, a similar discipline is required for communicating about one's qualifications to a potential employer. Anyone who has ever received a rambling resume for a job application knows why that's important. I remember receiving a resume from a person who was applying for the position of director of a tutoring center. The resume was several inches thick, with attachments that showed everything the person had ever done—most of it not related to the position in question. Moreover, some of it was trivial, giving [the] impression [the] person did not value depth. In short, no discipline had been used in culling and sorting the potential entries to address the position.

The focus on a specific audience and purpose also shapes the requirements for kinds of samples one will choose to include; audience and purpose also determine the criteria for quality of such a portfolio. For example, the portfolio used as part of the process for admission to student teaching at Alverno College specifies a number of entries that are considered "evidence" for readiness for student teaching—a videotape of a lesson with children or young adults, an analysis of that lesson, a sample of one's subject area focus, a piece of reflective writing, a sample of instructional materials one has created. The criteria make explicit the need to see integration of theory and practice, application of instructional principles, and sensitivity to diversity.

> The quality of a showcase portfolio is dependent upon thoughtful determination of the entries.

The quality of such a showcase portfolio is dependent upon thoughtful determination of the entries, given the constraints of certain types of entries required. In that it is like the sonnet—drawing flexibility and creativity from discipline. Of course, the portfolio is less rigidly defined than the sonnet—ordinarily there are not restrictions on size, media, or presentation and it allows for a range of formats.

One final point about the showcase portfolio. This type of portfolio, more than others, can be a relatively "high stakes" process. Something important may hinge upon it—admission to student teaching, selection for an art show, a job. Again, there is parallel to the sonnet or any literary work: is it good enough to publish?

I'd like to end this reflection on the portfolio as sonnet with another poem on the sonnet, this time from Keats, that says, in effect, let's take as much liberty as we need to in order to make the form serve its purpose. That's my advice, too, with respect to the portfolio.

> **On the Sonnet**
> *If by dull rhymes our English must be chained,*
> *And, like Andromeda, the sonnet sweet*
> *Fettered, in spite of pained loveliness,*
> *Let us find, if we must be constrained,*
> *Sandals more interwoven and complete*
> *To fit the naked foot of Poesy;*
> *Let us inspect the lyre, and weigh the stress*
> *Of every chord, and see what may be gained*
> *By ear industrious, and attention meet;*
> *Misers of sound and syllable, no less*
> *Than Midas of his coinage, let us be*
> *Jealous of dead leaves in the bay-wreath crown;*
> *So, if we may not let the Muse be free,*
> *She will be bound with garlands of her own.*
>   —John Keats 1819

The challenge for all of us engaged in the design of portfolio assessment is to assist our students to learn how to make their products more "interwoven and complete," weighing "the stress of every chord" to assure that the portfolio becomes an expression worthy of their—and our—time and effort. While the external focus implied in the image of portfolio as sonnet is important, other uses of the portfolio are equally and perhaps more important in teaching and learning. The functions that I call *mirror* and *map* will illustrate these approaches.

PORTFOLIO AS MIRROR

The mirror is a more obvious metaphor and I'm using it fairly literally to ask the question *how can the portfolio assist one to see oneself?* If we think about the ways in which one can *see* one's development, there are other images that come to mind as well. For physical development, an analog of the mirror is the photograph—we can go back through a collection of photographs to see our movement from infant to toddler to child to adolescent and on into adulthood. And most of us probably had a wall or a door in our house as we were growing up where our parents noted the changes in our height from year to year.

With intellectual, cognitive, and educational development the picture of one's growth over time is less apparent, especially if all you have as a record of that growth are test scores or grades. For some 20 years, the faculty at Alverno have been working with this question of making student development visible and accessible to the student, through video portfolios, written portfolios, and multimedia collections of work. We have discovered that there is a powerful impact on growth and self awareness when students can *see* their own development in speaking, in writing, in thinking and problem solving.

> There is a powerful impact on growth and self awareness when students can *see* their own development.

The ability to see development in these less visible areas requires clarity about what type of growth is important. Making clear what students need to know and be able to do, not only in a specific assignment or class, but across the experiences that lead to a college degree, is a necessary base. It requires clear criteria about what will *count* as meeting the goal that has been set. And it requires samples of performance over time so that learners and their teachers can look at how they have grown and changed.

The *developmental* portfolio is the kind of portfolio I think of when I think of the portfolio as mirror. For example, when students look at their writing over time in relationship to the expectations for clear writing, they recognize the learning that has occurred and they consolidate that learning. Think of the possibilities for self awareness available implicit in a study of several drafts of the same paper or of several papers over the course of a class or a year. The impact of recognizing one's growth can also be present in the process of putting together a showcase portfolio, when students review their work to choose the pieces they will include. As they complete their student teaching admission portfolios, our students often say "I didn't realize how much I had learned."

Because of its focus on development and progress, the developmental portfolio is relatively "low stakes." Students include more of a range of their work, showing the progress that they have made in a semester. They show the contrast between earlier drafts of a written work and the later, more polished, drafts. The goal is not selection of the best work, but a picture of the progress of learning.

The process of looking at one's development through a portfolio process functions like a literal mirror—when one see one's own image or performance— the *literal* reflection sparks *internal* reflection. If this is what my speaking looks like, what do I want to work on so that I can improve? What do I want to celebrate as something that shows me at my best? What provides a picture of where I have come through the learning process?

> **The goal is not selection of the best work, but a picture of the progress of learning.**

PORTFOLIO AS MAP

That last set of questions leads to the final image: portfolio as map. Clearly the map image is linked to the mirror—focusing on what you see can spark the question about where you want to go next. In the image of the map, a portfolio provides a framework for one to look at where next to set goals for one's own progress. The combination of samples of work and a sense of developmental criteria make the portfolio a tool to talk about growth and opportunities to develop further. Criteria for performance, such as the Alverno criteria for speaking across the curriculum, guide the interaction between student and teacher.

Students often begin their work with speaking by writing out everything that want to say. While this may help organize their thoughts, it prevents them from fully engaging with the audience, because their eyes must follow the text or lose the flow of the words. Even if a student memorizes a written speech the barrier with the audience remains, for it's hard to break away from a prepared text to deal with the questions one sees in the eyes of listeners. If a speaker does break away, then there is the difficulty of getting back into the text.

The description of the speaking ability at Alverno incorporates a quality called *speaking on your feet*. The criteria for this quality ask students to work at developing ways other than written text to prepare a speech. Faculty assist students to develop skill with a technique called mapping, outlining the flow of one's plan for a speech, without writing out every word. The map of a speech allows the speaker to interact with the audience, adjusting to the need for more clarification or less. The spontaneous nature of the delivery of a speech from a map provides a more natural voice pattern as well.

Students begin their careers as Alverno students with a speech during the entry assessment process. Because this it the entry level, the criterion related to "speaking on your feet" requires only that [students] "speak for at *least one minute* before an actual or imagined audience." In practice, the students speak before the camera person operating a video recorder. They view their speech during the first weeks of their first semester and get a sense of where they're starting from. As they move through the curriculum, the criteria for this aspect of speaking become more demanding:

• **Level 2:** Speaks on her feet (not reading or reciting) for a *recognizable portion* of the presentation

• **Level 3:** Speaks on her feet for *most* of the presentation

• **Level 4:** Gives the *consistent impression* of speaking *with* the audience.

Criteria specify a total of ten areas of speaking that students work to develop across the curriculum, e.g., reaching audience through structure, reaching audience through support and development, reaching audience through media, and reaching audience through appropriate content. Each have been spelled out in four developmental levels; the faculty have called these levels pedagogically developmental because they provide guidance to the student as they practice speaking about what they are learning.

At Alverno, our students' portfolios (e.g., the video portfolio for speaking, the writing portfolio, a collection of materials from the student's teacher preparation program) are made up of entries gathered from assignments and projects over time. The kind of work assigned thus makes a big difference. If students have only been asked to write in one mode or to one type of audience (or no audience except the implied teacher as audience), their portfolios will provide less opportunity to find direction. The role of the teacher in providing assignments that focus on the goals of the course and the program and projects that stretch the students' learning is critical.

Self assessment is the primary tool that makes the portfolio like a map. Using explicit criteria, the student develops the ability to look at her own work and determine the strengths and weaknesses evident in a particular performance or across a set of performances. She begins to set goals to address the areas she needs to develop and to deepen her areas of strength.

When made integral across the curriculum, the process of self-assessment and goal setting becomes an habitual practice. For example, Alverno students create formal, showcase portfolios for admission to student teaching. But they do not see these portfolios as "completed." During student teaching, they update or change entries to keep up with their current growth. They then begin to use the portfolio as a framework for ongoing professional development planning—where do I want to develop next? And they begin to set their own criteria for the quality they seek.

> We need to teach the process of reflection, particularly the kinds of questions that spark reflection.

The power of seeing the portfolio as map is to see that reflection can bring together the inner self and the outer world. The portfolio, as the theme of this conference suggests, encourages reflection—helping me to see my self and my strengths and weaknesses, but also to look at the sources of my growth in the larger world, especially the world of professional practice.

Reflection is not an automatic result of taking courses in the liberal arts. We need to teach the process of reflection, particularly the kinds of questions that spark reflection. At Alverno, we ask our students a number of question[s] to guide the development of reflection: "What connections can I make between what I'm learning in one class with what I'm learning in another?"; "What questions do I have about my learning?" Of course, the initial response of many is that "I don't have any questions." But when they hear the questions of others, they begin to realize how they might look more deeply.

Students don't initially know what to do with a sample of their own performance, such as a speaking performance. So we use explicit criteria to teach the process of self assessment as a first step toward reflection. We also model the kinds of questions they can ask about performance: "What did I like best about this performance? What would I do differently if I could do it over or when I do it again?" Over time, students gradually take responsibility for their own reflection, using the criteria provided by faculty. But they also begin to add additional frameworks to guide their reflection, drawing upon their developing philosophy of education. Ultimately, the highest "stakes" are those we set for ourselves. The portfolio as map captures the sense of a process made a habit of mind, of a commitment to ongoing professional growth.

PORTFOLIO AS SONNET, MIRROR AND MAP
Just as Wordsworth and Keats questioned the sonnet and probed the ways it could capture the expression of the poet, we need to continue as educators to question the portfolio and probe its potential. My fear is that too much attention may be paid to the form of the portfolio, without sufficient care given to its power for learning. That power is unleashed when teachers see the portfolio process as dependent upon the clarity of goals for student performance through their work in the liberal arts and professional education curriculum; when they attend to the quality of the assignments, projects and assessments that they provide for their students; and when they take the responsibility for teaching students the process of reflection and self assessment.

Both the sonnet and the portfolio are, indeed, a "scanty plot of ground." It's what we do [with] and how we use the portfolio that can make it a rich resource for reflection and growth.

Differentiated Evaluation in Professional Development Schools: An Alternative Paradigm for Preservice Teacher Evaluation

by Lucindia H. Chance and Thomas A. Rakes

Recent media reports have described a variety of education related problems including a number of issues involving teacher education and teacher licensure. The "Nation at Risk," the Holmes Group and others have expressed concern for public schools and higher education as well as offering ideas for the restructuring of these aged bureaucracies. Warnings from *Newsweek* in its feature article "The Failure of Teacher Education" (October, 1990), "Tomorrow's Schools" (Holmes, 1986), and "Research on Teacher Education" (Lainer and Little, 1986) all reflect a high level of concern for teacher education. Roth (1992) refers to two possible paradigms. One paradigm suggest[s] dismantling the current system of training teachers. The other paradigm offers a concept through which the current system could be reorganized to include much closer collaboration between K–12 and higher education as well as supporting the empowerment of K–12 teachers as a major part of the training/supervisory partnership that is closely associated with evaluating student teachers. The following discussion is based upon the evaluation process now in place in nine professional development schools including seven elementary, one middle and one high school. Specific attention is given to the overall con-

Paper presented at the CREATE National Evaluation Institute, Gatlinburg, Tennessee, July 10–15, 1994, ED 376 162. © 1994 by Lucindia H. Chance and Thomas A. Rakes. Reprinted with permission.

cept of portfolio evaluation in teacher education and how differentiated evaluation can be conducted.

The concept and operational guidelines of professional development schools vary widely across the nation. Developed around a collaborative focus (Oja, 1990–91), The University of Memphis Professional Development Schools are based on the concept of true partners engaged in simultaneous renewal of teacher education in selected PreK–12 schools. The collaborative model includes team teaching at both levels, peer curriculum projects, joint research and a valued partnership in teacher training and PreK–12 education.

> The concept and operational guidelines of professional development schools vary widely across the nation.

A DIFFERENTIATED MODEL OF EVALUATION

Cooperating Teachers and a Portfolio System

The collaborative model is based on the idea that classroom teachers can become an equal partner with University Liaisons in the supervision of student teachers. In practice, classroom teachers may be in a better position than their university peers to be of practical assistance to preservice teachers. This concept of teacher-based empowerment enables K–12 teachers, through the use of a differentiated evaluation system, to take a major responsibility for evaluating student teachers. After a training period, cooperating teachers should be prepared to play a legitimate role in determining who meets the standards associated with student teaching and then, recommend alternatives for those who are or are not prepared to teach.

Historically, supervisory and professional licensure roles have been controlled by the university and individual state licensure/certification agencies. During the early 1980s state legislatures passed some 700 pieces of legislation in nearly every state. Based on feedback from student teachers, classroom teachers, and teacher educators, many states have increased the number of student teaching practicum weeks. Although extended time in the classroom is desirable, the quality of the supervision and evaluation provided by the cooperating teacher is as much an issue as the amount of time spent in a placement. Two critical elements of this preparedness include a knowledge of clinical supervision techniques and an understanding of how to evaluate teaching.

An understanding of what needs to be done to guide, support and evaluate a student teacher is not typically a part of a classroom teacher's training. Few professional development activities involve information on the role of cooperating teachers. In a recent study Andrews reported on authentic assessment as an integrated activity in methods classes (Andrews, 1993–94). The target of our discussion involves a concept of portfolio evaluation which is one element of a

> **Few professional development activities involve information on the role of cooperating teachers.**

broader evaluation concept commonly referred to as "authentic" assessment which we have operationalized in a student teaching setting. The use of a portfolio system is a part of an overall belief that authentic assessment should be a part of the overall student teaching process. Customarily, authentic assessment is described as a content based process commonly associated with a teaching area such as the teaching of reading (Valencia, Hiebert, and Afflerbach, 1994). The following discussion deals with how one particular system of authentic assessment can be used in teacher education, the Practice Teaching Portfolio. For our purposes, the particular portfolio currently in use in the College of Education at the University of Memphis will be described.

Consisting of three major sections, the folder style document includes a front page section with directions and demographic data including dates of placement conferences and other information. There are also three signature lines for the student teacher, cooperating teacher, and the University Liaison to sign off after three post-teaching conferences. The inside two pages provide for evaluating, on a five point scale, the student teacher in the following areas: (1) planning; (2) communication; (3) leadership; (4) teaching strategies; (5) classroom management; and (6) evaluation. Provision is made in this section for the student teacher to complete a self-rating early during the the placement period. Table One shows a sample section. The back of the folder has three blocked areas for comments during the term of a placement.

Table 1
Sample From Practice Teaching Portfolio

KEYS TO RATING SCALES

Progress Reports	*Final Evaluation*
1, 2: Needs Improvement	1, 2: Inadequate
3, 4: Developing	3, 4: Meets Performance Expectations
5: Practicing	5: Exceeds Performance Expectations
N/A: Not Applicable	N/A: Not Applicable

Editor's note:
CT = cooperating teacher
US = university supervisor

SELF EVALUATION	PROGRESS REPORT 2		FINAL EVALUATION		
	CT	US	CT	US	
___	___	___	___	___	**TEACHING STRATEGIES** Knowledge of subject matter.
___	___	___	___	___	Provides purpose and description of learning task.
___	___	___	___	___	Provides learners practice and review and includes all students in learning process.
___	___	___	___	___	Establishes and maintains learner involvement by adapting instruction to the learning pace and understanding of students.
___	___	___	___	___	Uses instructional time effectively and efficiently.
___	___	___	___	___	Incorporates problem solving and thinking skills.
___	___	___	___	___	Selects a variety of instructional or media materials.
___	___	___	___	___	Uses teacher created and developed materials.

In addition to the use of the reporting mechanism on the portfolio itself, it is beneficial to gather a variety of additional information which can be placed in the portfolio through the placement period. Evidence involving at least five observations in classrooms other than the assigned placement, a typed unit lesson plan (approved and initialed by the cooperating teacher), a sample lesson plan (approved and initialed by the cooperating

Table 2
Sample Entries in Three Different Student Teaching Logs

September 1993   **Sample A**

Today I saw something that I knew I would see eventually, but I don't know if I was ready to deal with it. A little girl in the class, who has misbehaved a little, had her mother called by my cooperating teacher. She showed up at school today with her arm all bruised up, she said she got "a whopping" because my cooperating teacher had called her mother.

October 1993   **Sample B**

I am beginning to get used to the younger children now. The thing that amazes me about 3rd graders is their honesty. They tell everything they know about everyone they know. I overheard something very amusing today and felt certain it was an accurate account.

September 1993   **Sample C**

I was so nervous worrying about things (do I have everything, will I forget and leave something that I have planned out, etc.) that I woke up at 3:30 a.m. That's not good because today is my long day. After school I have to go to the student teaching seminar. It's gonna be a long day.

I'm using this time in class to write in my journal while the students are writing in theirs.

I got my free-be evaluation today. After I finished my lesson I just wanted to cry. The children had problems understanding the concept I was teaching (place value). I felt like a failure.

But my cooperating teacher and university supervisor kept telling me that is how it is in the real world of teaching. Some days they just don't get it the first time. That's why we learn to reteach.

I think I understand but I just wish it would have been on another day (one that I wasn't being evaluated [on]). I also need to learn how to control the behavior of the children better.

teacher), and other work samples or documents as determined by the cooperating teacher should all be included. Completion of a daily log is also required for each student teacher.

Student teaching logs include a narrative or anecdotal record/description of feelings and reactions at the end of each day of the placement. Copies of specific journal procedures are available from the authors. The logs are maintained separately (not in the portfolio) by the student teacher and submitted to the university at the conclusion of the placement. The purpose of the log is to assist student teachers in expressing their feelings and perceptions on paper and to hopefully show a progression of growth in confidence, comfort, and understanding of the teaching process. The logs are reviewed throughout the placement period, perhaps every two weeks, by the University Liaison. Student teaching logs are not to be used directly as a part of the evaluation but as a source of information for the University Liaison. See Table Two on page 31 for examples of three different student teachers' entries in their logs.

While each cooperating teacher maintains the portfolio and meets jointly with the student teacher and University Liaison, the University Liaison is making evaluative judgments using a different procedure called the "Snapshot Evaluation."

University Liaisons and Snapshot Evaluations
While the cooperating teacher is responsible for conducting three formal evaluations, the University Liaison is involved in a different process of observation. The snapshot evaluation procedure, Elementary Classroom Observation Measure, is a modified version of a procedure used by school administrators during the early 1980s and was most recently used to evaluate the effectiveness of federally funded programs for at-risk learners (Center for Research in Educational Policy, 1990). This procedure requires the University Liaison to conduct nine unannounced, five minute visits of the student teacher during a ten week placement period. During a five week placement, five snapshot observations would be expected. Using a very structured instrument, the snapshot observation involves noting a range of specific classroom occurrences within a five minute interval.

In Part One the snapshot instrument contains six major sections and calls for the user to first sketch a view of the classroom setup showing the placement of desks and work areas. Section B contains a checklist of items for a resource inventory (e.g., magazines, television, trade books, sink, maps, computer, puzzles, etc.). Part Two, classroom make-up and physical environment, contains sections for logging in each visit by month, day, and year along with a section requiring the user to list demographic information about the students, seating, classroom appearance and noise level. The main section of the instrument contains two recordkeeping pages with three different sections

Table 3
Sample from "Snapshot" Evaluation Form

Adult Behaviors

Behavior	Teacher	Other Adult
Explain (provide information)	① ② ③ ④ ⑤ ⑥ ⑦ ⑧ ⑨	① ② ③ ④ ⑤ ⑥ ⑦ ⑧ ⑨
Questioning	① ② ③ ④ ⑤ ⑥ ⑦ ⑧ ⑨	① ② ③ ④ ⑤ ⑥ ⑦ ⑧ ⑨
Answer questions	① ② ③ ④ ⑤ ⑥ ⑦ ⑧ ⑨	① ② ③ ④ ⑤ ⑥ ⑦ ⑧ ⑨
Lead group activity	① ② ③ ④ ⑤ ⑥ ⑦ ⑧ ⑨	① ② ③ ④ ⑤ ⑥ ⑦ ⑧ ⑨
Direct ongoing work	① ② ③ ④ ⑤ ⑥ ⑦ ⑧ ⑨	① ② ③ ④ ⑤ ⑥ ⑦ ⑧ ⑨
Correct/grade	① ② ③ ④ ⑤ ⑥ ⑦ ⑧ ⑨	① ② ③ ④ ⑤ ⑥ ⑦ ⑧ ⑨
Provide feedback	① ② ③ ④ ⑤ ⑥ ⑦ ⑧ ⑨	① ② ③ ④ ⑤ ⑥ ⑦ ⑧ ⑨
Test	① ② ③ ④ ⑤ ⑥ ⑦ ⑧ ⑨	① ② ③ ④ ⑤ ⑥ ⑦ ⑧ ⑨
Facilitate discussion	① ② ③ ④ ⑤ ⑥ ⑦ ⑧ ⑨	① ② ③ ④ ⑤ ⑥ ⑦ ⑧ ⑨
Oversee	① ② ③ ④ ⑤ ⑥ ⑦ ⑧ ⑨	① ② ③ ④ ⑤ ⑥ ⑦ ⑧ ⑨
Read to students	① ② ③ ④ ⑤ ⑥ ⑦ ⑧ ⑨	① ② ③ ④ ⑤ ⑥ ⑦ ⑧ ⑨
Transition time	① ② ③ ④ ⑤ ⑥ ⑦ ⑧ ⑨	① ② ③ ④ ⑤ ⑥ ⑦ ⑧ ⑨
Manage/give directions	① ② ③ ④ ⑤ ⑥ ⑦ ⑧ ⑨	① ② ③ ④ ⑤ ⑥ ⑦ ⑧ ⑨
Control/discipline	① ② ③ ④ ⑤ ⑥ ⑦ ⑧ ⑨	① ② ③ ④ ⑤ ⑥ ⑦ ⑧ ⑨
Prepare materials	① ② ③ ④ ⑤ ⑥ ⑦ ⑧ ⑨	① ② ③ ④ ⑤ ⑥ ⑦ ⑧ ⑨
Observe/listen	① ② ③ ④ ⑤ ⑥ ⑦ ⑧ ⑨	① ② ③ ④ ⑤ ⑥ ⑦ ⑧ ⑨
Encroachment	① ② ③ ④ ⑤ ⑥ ⑦ ⑧ ⑨	① ② ③ ④ ⑤ ⑥ ⑦ ⑧ ⑨
Not present	① ② ③ ④ ⑤ ⑥ ⑦ ⑧ ⑨	① ② ③ ④ ⑤ ⑥ ⑦ ⑧ ⑨

for noting subject observed and orientations (teacher-led, small group, independent, etc.), adult behaviors (36 items), and student behaviors (38 items) under teacher and student directed headings. See Table Three on page 33 for a sample from the adult behaviors section.

The next two pages of the form contain 16 and 13 items each and provide an opportunity to summarize the previous two pages using a four and a three point scale. Two major categories are listed: Teacher (student teacher) behaviors and Overall observations. The final page is allocated to space for the University Liaison to enter notes for each visit. This section is particularly help[ful] to explain unexpected or possibly misleading events such as "observed preparation for lunch" or "observed the aftermath of a clean-up following an art lesson." In some instances the discrete entries noted for specific categories during one five minute observation may provide misleading information if some reference as to what was observed is not provided. It is also useful to plan snapshot visits at different times during the day as well as spaced throughout the placement period.

> It is useful to plan snapshot visits at different times during the day as well as spaced throughout the placement period.

The use of snapshot evaluations add[s] an additional dimension to the overall portfolio process since the completed snapshot evaluation form is also included in each student teacher's completed portfolio. The use of the snapshot process does not preclude supervisors' making longer observations or their participation in demonstration or team teaching. Joint conferences among the student teacher, cooperating teacher, and the University Liaison are recommended but using different data gathering techniques for the cooperating [teacher] and supervisor.

Applying the concept of a collaborative evaluation process not only creates a more thorough evaluation of student teachers but also provides for a visible, concrete manner through which student teaching performance can be monitored. By combining the use of full lesson observations, snapshot evaluations, logs, related classroom observations, along with lesson and unit plans, an authentic record can be developed. Other elements could be added, such as video taped teaching segments or student teacher generated plans or projects. The purpose of using differentiated evaluation procedures is to do a better job evaluating student teachers and ultimately enhance their own overall level of performance.

BIBLIOGRAPHY

Andrews, W. D. E. (1993–94). Infusing authentic assessment into teacher education programs. *SRATE Journal, 3*(1), 3–7.

Center for Research in Educational Policy (1990). *Elementary Classroom Observation Measure.* Memphis, Tennessee, Memphis State University.

The failure of teacher education. (1990). *Newsweek,* 116(14), 58–60.

The Holmes Group. (1986). *Tomorrow's teachers: A report of the Holmes Group.* East Lansing, Michigan: The Holmes Group, Inc., *Resources in Education,* ED 270-454.

Lainer, J. E., & Little, J. W. (1986). Research on teacher education, in *Handbook of Research on Teaching,* M. C. Wittrock, Ed., New York: Macmillan.

Oja, S. N. (1990–91). The dynamics of collaboration: A collaborative approach to supervision in a five year teacher education program. *Action in Teacher Education,* 7(4), 11–20.

Roth, R. A. (1992). Dichotomous paradigms for teacher education: The rise or fall of the empire. *Action in Teacher Education,* 14(1), 1–9.

Valencia, S. W., Hiebert, E. H., & Afflerbach, P. P. (1994). *Authentic reading assessment: Practices and possibilities.* Newark, Delaware: International Reading Association.

Professional Development Journey: The Formative Plan

Developing and implementing a teacher portfolio program requires planning, time, patience, organization, and cooperation from students, teachers, and principals.—Peggy Perkins and Jeffrey Gelfer

ducators who have implemented portfolios in their own classrooms find that, as a result, students spend more time reflecting on their learning and self-assessing their work. Mary Dietz, citing Brooks and Grennon-Brooks, states that learning theories that apply to children can apply to adults as well. Using a constructive model for teaching and being aware of the learner's readiness for change play a vital role in the effectiveness of professional development. Many teachers and administrators realize that if portfolios can help students become more involved in their learning, they can also be used to help educators become more involved in their own professional growth.

The articles in this section address using the professional portfolio as a formative tool to improve classroom teaching. Each of the authors describes successful methods that districts, consortiums, or schools have used to create a professional portfolio system that invites "teachers to become the architects of their own professional development" (Wolf 1996). Some of the common elements in the systems discussed include encouraging educators to set their own goals, collecting evidence to document progress in meeting those goals, reflecting on their learnings, collaborating with peers throughout the process, and sharing the final product with other professionals.

Kenneth Wolf, in his article "Developing an Effective Teaching Portfolio," recommends organizing a teaching portfolio into three categories: (1) background information; (2) teaching artifacts and reflections; and (3) professional information. He discusses his belief that a teaching portfolio should be more than just a scrapbook of heart-warming mementos but instead "should carefully and thoughtfully document a set of accomplishments attained over an extended period. And, it should be an ongoing process conducted in the company of mentors and colleagues."

In the article "Using Portfolios as a Framework for Professional Development," Mary Dietz discusses the need for teachers to clarify their purposes for the portfolio and formulate their "credo" or basic values and belief system that drive their decisions as teachers *before* they begin collecting evidence. Dietz argues that teachers must identify a focus for learning, collect evidence, and collaborate with peers to develop their portfolio plan. She also emphasizes the link between each teacher's individual plan and the goals of other professionals at the school. She states, "The professional development portfolio provides teachers with a framework for initiating, planning, and facilitating their professional development while building connections between their professional goals and those of the school."

The importance of "purpose" figures prominently in these discussions of professional portfolio systems. In many of the articles, authors advocate having teachers select one or two major goals for the year; for example, if a teacher selects authentic assessment as a goal, all the artifacts included (rubrics, observation checklists, student portfolios) would provide evidence of significant progress toward assessing students more authentically. Other authors, however, recommend using a portfolio to document the competencies included in most classroom observations.

For example, Peggy Perkins and Jeffrey Gelfer, in their article "Portfolio Assessment of Teachers," discuss how teachers could collect evidence throughout the year to document that they are proficient in the following eight competencies: (1) content and curriculum coverage; (2) methodology and classroom organization; (3) instructional planning; (4) classroom management; (5) communication skills; (6) evaluation of students; (7) use of resources; and (8) professionalism. They recommend that each week faculty members select the best representations of their work to put in their portfolios, review these pieces again at the end of the month to remove contents that seem redundant or unrepresentative of their work, and then, at the end of the year, reflect on their growth and progress in meeting the competencies.

The final article in this section, "Scholarship Reconsidered: A Challenge to Use Teaching Portfolios to Document the Scholarship of Teaching," describes how portfolios could be used at the university level to document scholarship and to "increase the dialogue on teaching by helping to create conversations" among mentors and colleagues, members of an evaluation committee, or members of committees that interview and hire teachers. The author, Don Boileau, describes three types of materials that could be included in a scholarship portfolio: (1) products of good teaching; (2) one's own materials; and (3) materials from others. He recommends that universities ask prospective teachers for evidence of their teaching effectiveness during the interview process, stating that "the portfolio is becoming a nationally acceptable way of documenting teaching activity."

It is evident that professional portfolios can significantly improve staff development by giving teachers time to synthesize ideas, experiment with strategies, and apply educational theories. Teachers will also be able to make some long-term transfer by applying what they have learned and reflecting on "what works" and "what doesn't work." As Dietz states,

> Schools that are ready to make a commitment to professional development for teachers that extends beyond the usual training sessions seem to find that the professional development portfolio enhances and extends their professional development efforts with teachers.

Developing an Effective Teaching Portfolio

by Kenneth Wolf

ducators have used student portfolios to assess student performance for many years. Recently, they have turned their attention to portfolios for teachers (Shulman 1988).

Why the interest in teaching portfolios? Although portfolios can be time-consuming to construct and cumbersome to review, they also can capture the complexities of professional practice in ways that no other approach can. Not only are they an effective way to assess teaching quality, but they also provide teachers with opportunities for self-reflection and collegial interactions based on documented episodes of their own teaching.

Essentially, a teaching portfolio is a collection of information about a teacher's practice. It can include a variety of information, such as lesson plans, student assignments, teachers' written descriptions and videotapes of their instruction, and formal evaluations by supervisors. If not carefully thought out, however, a portfolio can easily take the form of a scrapbook or steamer trunk. The "scrapbook" portfolio is a collection of eye-catching and heart warming mementos that has strong personal meaning for the portfolio owner. The "steamer trunk" portfolio is a large container filled to the brim with assorted papers and projects.

Unfortunately, these kinds of portfolios do not allow for serious self-reflection, and others cannot examine them in an informed way. They do not illustrate an underlying philosophy of teaching, and they provide no information about instructional goals or teaching context. They do not explain the con-

From *Educational Leadership*, vol. 53, no. 6, March 1996, pp. 34–37. © 1996 by the Association for Supervision and Curriculum Development. Reprinted with permission.

tents of the portfolio or connect them to intended instructional outcomes. Perhaps most important, such portfolios contain no written reflections by the creators on their teaching experiences.

A teaching portfolio should be more than a miscellaneous collection of artifacts or an extended list of professional activities. It should carefully and thoughtfully document a set of accomplishments attained over an extended period. And, it should be an ongoing process conducted in the company of mentors and colleagues.

WHY DEVELOP A PORTFOLIO?

Teachers create portfolios for a variety of reasons. In teacher education programs, students develop portfolios to demonstrate their achievement. Later, they may present these portfolios at job interviews. Experienced teachers construct portfolios to become eligible for bonuses and advanced certification. And, some administrators have invited teachers to become architects of their own professional development by having them create portfolios based on individual growth plans.

> A teaching portfolio should be more than a miscellaneous collection of artifacts or an extended list of professional activities.

In Colorado, for example, teachers are preparing portfolios in many different settings. In the Douglas County School District south of Denver, teachers submit portfolios to demonstrate their teaching excellence. Those who meet district standards receive annual performance bonuses. Some teachers also are striving to earn national recognition by preparing portfolios for the National Board of Professional Teaching Standards. And soon, Colorado will require all educators, including administrators, to develop portfolios in order to renew their professional licenses.

SELECTING THE CONTENTS

A portfolio might include items such as lesson plans, anecdotal records, student projects, class newsletters, videotapes, annual evaluations, letters of recommendation, and the like. It is important, however, to carefully select the contents of the finished portfolio so that it is manageable, both for the person who constructs it and for those who will review it.

Figure 1
How to Organize a Teaching Portfolio

Table of Contents

I.   *Background Information*
  - Resumé
  - Background Information on Teacher and Teaching Context
  - Educational Philosophy and Teaching Goals

II. *Teaching Artifacts and Reflections*
  Documentation of an Extended Teaching Activity
  - Overview of Unit Goals and Instructional Plan
  - List of Resources Used in Unit
  - Two Consecutive Lesson Plans
  - Videotape of Teaching
  - Student Work Samples
  - Evaluation of Student Work
  - Reflective Commentary by the Teacher
  - Additional Units/Lessons/Student Work as Appropriate

III. *Professional Information*
  - List of Professional Activities
  - Letters of Recommendation
  - Formal Evaluations

While the specific form and content of a portfolio can vary depending upon its purpose, most portfolios contain some combination of teaching artifacts and written reflections. These are the heart of the portfolio. The introductory section, in which the teacher broadly describes his or her teaching philosophy and goals, and the concluding section, which contains evidence of ongoing professional development and formal evaluations, provide a frame for these artifacts and reflections. (Figure 1 provides a suggested outline for organizing a teaching portfolio.)

Here's (in part) how Susan Howard, a pre-service elementary school teacher at the University of Colorado at Denver, described her philosophy of teaching:

> Visitors to my classroom would see a supportive, risk-free environment in which the students have an active voice in their learning and in classroom decision making. Students would be

engaged in a variety of individual and collaborative work designed to accommodate their diverse learning styles. Curriculum would combine basic skills, authentic learning, and critical thinking. Finally, visitors also would see parental involvement demonstrated in a variety of ways. . . .

Students should help establish class rules, have a vote in the topics for the year, and have a voice in as much of their learning as possible. I believe it is important to use a variety of presentation styles and provide a range of learning experiences to support students' diverse learning styles. . . .

In my classroom, language arts would pair phonics with literature enrichment. Math would combine basic skills and application. Science and social studies would emphasize application and problem-solving exercises while targeting basic area knowledge.

I would invite parents to share information about hobbies, skills, jobs, and cultures. I would communicate with them frequently, and would encourage them to become involved in their child's learning in as many ways as possible.

Artifacts (unit plans, student work samples) are essential ingredients in a teaching portfolio, but they must be framed with explanations. For example, Linda Lovino, a high school English teacher from the Douglas County School District, included surveys of students, parents, and colleagues in the portfolio she submitted for the Outstanding Teacher Program. She commented in her portfolio on what she learned from these surveys:

I felt validated when the client surveys indicated that my students and their parents feel I use a variety of teaching strategies and methods, and that I am knowledgeable in my subject area. Although I received high ratings from over 80 percent of parents and students on the statements, "The teacher effectively communicates information regarding growth and progress of my child," and "The teacher effectively motivates the student," the remaining 20 percent of the respondents gave me a "neutral" rating.

I feel these areas are essential to being an outstanding teacher. Therefore, I am currently researching and developing methods that might help me better motivate students and assess their progress.

Figure 2
Sample Portfolio Caption

Title: Weekly Classroom Newsletter

Date: March 15, 1996

Name: John Stanford

Description of Context:
Students write, edit, and publish this weekly newsletter in writer's workshop.

Interpretation:
This newsletter is one way that I keep parents informed about classroom events. It is also an example of how I engage students in meaningful learning activities.

Additional Comments:
Parents have told me how they use the newsletter to talk with their children about what is happening in school. I also learn more about what my students find important or newsworthy in class each week!

This is an example of the kind of captions Colorado teachers use in License Renewal Portfolios.

Each artifact also should be accompanied by a brief statement, or caption, which identifies it and describes the context in which it was created. This often can be done in one or two sentences. Figure 2 shows the kinds of captions Colorado educators include in their license renewal portfolios.

Reflective commentaries are another important part of the portfolio. These commentaries do more than describe the portfolio contents; they examine the teaching documented in the portfolio and reflect on what teacher and students learn.

Valerie Wheeler, a middle school teacher from Boulder, included an account of a unit she taught on communicable diseases in the portfolio she submitted to the National Board for Professional Teaching Standards:

> The primary goal for teaching about communicable diseases is to educate students about their own role in leading a safe and healthy life. . . . When young people are informed, chances are they will act in ways that protect their own and others' health.

> The day I introduced this topic to my students, we used the entire period to discuss the meaning of the term "communicable disease." Together, we brainstormed questions about disease—its history, status, and future.
>
> As in most class discussions, students eventually began to share relevant personal or family experiences. The energy and participation level was high, and by the end of class, two themes had emerged. Students wanted to know more about the most common communicable diseases, and they wanted to know more about AIDS.
>
> Because student understanding is enhanced by prior experiences, I assigned each student to write a brief history of his or her own health.

In addition to the written account, Valerie included a videotape of her teaching along with samples of her teaching materials and her students' work. These included a newspaper article about the rights of tuberculosis patients, which her students had read and annotated; a letter they wrote to the mayor about the confinement of TB patients; thank you letters to guest speakers from the local AIDS center; and photographs of a quilt the class made after reading about the AIDS quilt.

DEVELOPING YOUR PROFILE

There are many approaches to developing a teaching portfolio. The following one involves articulating an educational philosophy and identifying goals, building and refining the portfolio, and framing the contents for presentation to others.

• Explain your educational philosophy and teaching goals. Describe in broad strokes the key principles that underlie your practice. These principles will help you select goals for your portfolio.

• Choose specific features of your instructional program to document. Collect a wide range of artifacts, and date and annotate them so you will remember important details when assembling the final portfolio. Consider keeping a journal for written reflections on your teaching.

• Collaborate with a mentor and other colleagues. This is an essential, but often overlooked, part of the process. Ideally, your mentor will have experience both in teaching and in portfolio construction. And consider meeting at regular intervals to discuss your teaching and your portfolio with a group of colleagues.

• Assemble your portfolio in a form that others can readily examine. While any number of containers will work, the easiest to organize and handle seems to be a loose-leaf notebook. (Electronic portfolios may soon replace notebooks.)

• Assess the portfolio. Assessment can range from an informal self-assessment to formal scoring by the National Board for Professional Teaching Standards. Such assessments are tied to specific performance standards. (The Douglas County School District in Colorado has identified three categories, each of which contains specific criteria, for assessing outstanding teachers: assessment and instruction, content and pedagogy, and collaboration and partnership.)

A MEANS TO AN END

Portfolios have much to offer the teaching profession. When teachers carefully examine their own practices, those practices are likely to improve. The examples of accomplished practice that portfolios provide also can be studied and adapted for use in other classrooms.

Too often, good teaching vanishes without a trace because we have no structure or tradition for preserving the best of what teachers do. Portfolios allow teachers to retain examples of good teaching so they can examine them, talk about them, adapt them, and adopt them.

Finally, it is important to remember that the objective is not to create outstanding portfolios, but rather to cultivate outstanding teaching and learning.

REFERENCE

Shulman, L. S. 1988. A union of insufficiencies: Strategies for teacher assessment in a period of reform. *Educational Leadership* 46 (3): 36–41.

Using Portfolios as a Framework for Professional Development

by Mary E. Dietz

T eachers can prepare professional development portfolios and use the portfolio materials as a means to facilitate their learning and to improve their classroom practices. This article offers a brief history and description of the professional development portfolio. Included are how and why it was developed, the theoretical foundations that drove the design, and the practical experiences of teachers as learners that were incorporated in the design.

We will also share how teachers have used the professional development portfolio and the lessons learned from working with them. The concluding section will provide insights into the influence of the professional development portfolio on teachers as learners and into their implications for the design of staff development.

HISTORY AND BACKGROUND

Interest in using professional development portfolios as a means to facilitate teachers' learning and increase the impact of professional development on classroom practices began in June 1987 as a result of a Professional Development Consortium project in San Diego, California. Mariam True, the director of the Consortium, wanted to create a process for helping teachers define their professional development needs.

From *Journal of Staff Development*, vol. 16, no. 2, Spring 1995, pp. 40–43.
© 1995 by the National Staff Development Council. Reprinted with permission of the National Staff Development Council, POB 240, Oxford, Ohio 45056, 513-523-6029.

She wanted staff development offerings to be learner-centered and to engage teachers in learning and integrating innovations. This could be accomplished, she believed, if teachers had opportunities to make informed decisions regarding the focus of their learning and had time and opportunity for collaboration.

> Many school districts were seeking alternative assessments for teachers who were participating in study groups or peer coaching.

After the concept of the professional development portfolio was developed at the Consortium, it was implemented at 12 sites throughout Imperial, San Diego, and Orange Counties in California. The process was very effective in inviting and focusing teachers' involvement in their learning process.

In addition, many school districts were seeking alternative assessments for teachers who were participating in study groups or peer coaching. In a very short amount of time, requests were being made to use the portfolio as an alternative to traditional teacher evaluation at the 12 sites.

One of the other districts trying the portfolio process was the Orange County (Orlando, Florida) Public Schools, which in 1993 began using the portfolio with 150 teachers and 35 administrators. The portfolio process has had a positive impact on building collegial cultures and helping teachers examine the role of assessment in their classrooms.

What is a Portfolio?
There are three types of portfolios (Dietz, 1994):
• *Presentation Portfolio*—a collection, resume, or album that represents an individual's accomplishments, learning, strengths, and expertise. It can serve as an introduction for personal and professional opportunities, highlighting the purpose and meaning of one's work.
• *Working Portfolio*—a collection of assignments, artifacts, and other evidence that fulfills prescribed competencies, standards, or outcomes. Outcomes for credentialling, course participation, or other requirements are established by mediators, teachers, or supervisors of one's work.

• *Learner Portfolio*—an envelope of the mind (a reflection of knowledge, experiences, and feelings) that provides a framework and process for the learner to focus learning, collect artifacts and evidence, and describe their learning outcomes.

The professional development portfolio is a combination of the working portfolio and the learner portfolio with the teacher as "learner" making the decisions about the focus and design for learning. The professional development portfolio provides teachers with a framework for initiating, planning, and facilitating their professional development while building connections between their professional goals and those of the school (Dietz, 1994).

ASSUMPTIONS ABOUT THE PORTFOLIO

Learning theory can help define the philosophy that guides the portfolio process. The design is built on the following assumptions:

1. Professional development activities are most effective when professionals set their own goals, determine a preferred method for learning, and make decisions about how to best integrate new learning (Krupp, 1987).

2. Teachers will engage in learning if they are involved in the process of discovering innovations in teaching and in collegial sharing, empowered to build a plan that will support their goals, encouraged to question current assumptions and explore new findings while gaining expertise, and are responsible for agreed-upon outcomes (Glasser, 1993).

3. Professional growth of teachers is critical to the process of change in schools (Joyce, 1990).

4. Change is a process of resocialization that takes place over time and that requires interaction. Partner meetings and peer-to-peer word of mouth are the most effective methods for initiating substantive change (Dietz, 1993).

5. Learning theories that apply to children have validity for adult learners as well. Using a constructivist model for teaching and being aware of the learner's readiness for change, in addition to considering where the learner is in his or her career cycle, play a vital role in the ultimate success of professional development (Brooks & Grennon-Brooks, 1987).

HOW TEACHERS USE THE PORTFOLIOS

The professional development portfolio is based on four features:

- *Purpose*—examining the reason why you are putting together a Professional Development Portfolio;
- *Focus*—determining your "entry point" or theme for learning;
- *Process*—deciding how you will collaborate, learn, build a plan, and reflect; and
- *Outcomes*—selecting concluding remarks, rethinking, and preparing exhibitions that describe learning.

All four feature[s] interact and are interdependent. They contribute to the building of a professional development plan, a core component of the portfolio that will be facilitated by collaboration, reflection, and professional development activities (Dietz, 1994).

> **Participants begin the [professional development portfolio] process by clarifying their purposes for the portfolio and formulating their *credo*.**

The portfolio itself consists of a structured journal (a journal with sentences to be completed and/or questions to be reflected on), a folder for artifacts and evidences, a zipper bag, and an optional reflective journal (has blank pages to process reflective thinking). The process begins with a half-day session, conducted by a facilitator familiar with the portfolio process, to introduce the portfolio. Teachers participate in activities to construct a conceptual understanding of the portfolio. They learn techniques for coaching and reflection, which are used throughout the portfolio process.

Participants begin the process by clarifying their purposes for the portfolio and formulating their *credo*—their basic values and belief systems that drive their decisions and learning as teachers. Next, they write about their focus for learning as they identify areas of greatest interest and/or concern.

After the teachers have identified a focus for learning that creates a context for their inquiry, they meet with their portfolio partners and discuss activities they might include in their professional development plan. Portfolio partners are usually peers, partners for team teaching, or study group colleagues.

It is helpful if portfolio partners are in close proximity so that classroom visits and time to collaborate are more easily scheduled. In most instances, teachers select their partners. During the school year, they continue to add comments and share them with their partners as they work through their plans. The portfolio is designed to encourage teachers to look for changes in goals and interests as they continue to collaborate.

> **Throughout the entire process, teachers meet with their partners for 30 minutes every other week.**

Throughout the entire process, teachers meet with their partners for 30 minutes every other week. They share learning and reflections from experiences with students and from the professional development activities specified in their plan.

These meetings are good opportunities to asses what is working and what needs improvement, to revisit goals, and to add new activities to their plans. These brief meetings with partners also provide opportunities to plan for and discuss new instructional practices and curriculum as the teachers sift through the artifacts and evidence they have collected and share outcomes from recent professional development activities.

Professional development activities might include:
- Visiting local schools and other educational institutions.
- Participating in workshops or courses.
- Observing others teaching one's own class.
- Developing hobbies and talents that contribute to work.
- Meeting with others who have had experience and expertise in areas of interest.
- Studying research and experiences other have had with innovations.
- Receiving feedback of one's own teaching by a partner or another colleague.
- Videotaping one's own teaching to observe the teaching or to share with a colleague, inviting additional perspectives and feedback.

BENEFITS OF THE PROCESS
The portfolio informs continuous learning and provides a structure for:
1. Focusing learning.
2. Building a growth plan.
3. Collecting artifacts and evidence.
4. Facilitating collegial relationships.
5. Sharpening skills and abilities.
6. Reflecting on learning.
7. Drawing on past experiences and knowledge.
8. Observing students' learning.

Positive results have occurred in schools using the professional development portfolio process, particularly in Orange County, Florida. Evaluation of the effectiveness of the portfolio process in that district revealed:
• The collaboration opportunities resulted in new teaching teams.
• Teachers tried innovations and collaborative techniques they would not ordinarily have tried.
• Teachers used alternative assessment techniques with their students.
• Teachers became more aware of the learning process for themselves and their students.
• Administrators were more aware of classroom practices and needs.
• Teachers self-evaluated and informed their administrators about their growth.
• Partner meetings and study groups helped to keep the learning focus in the forefront for the entire team.
• Teachers and administrators made informed decisions regarding professional development opportunities.

SITES CURRENTLY INVOLVED IN THE PROCESS
The professional development portfolio [is] being used in a number of sites:
• Of the four high schools from California's Southern Consortium that are using the portfolio, two have received grants for school reform efforts and use the portfolio to assist them in program planning and monitoring success. Initial re-

sponses from teachers have been favorable. The greatest concerns are about the long-term commitment of school leadership to continue the process.

• The staff at a school in Imperial County, California, has eliminated formal evaluations for teachers who have had three or more outstanding evaluations. Instead these teachers will use the professional development portfolio to set their goals for the school term; participants are considering submitting a video at the end of the term which would illustrate their use of favorite innovative instructional practices.

• Several of the California Beginning Teacher Support and Assessment (BTSA) projects have selected this portfolio design as an organizer for facilitating feedback and continuous learning. They have found it helpful in defining and directing the coach/mentor role in the support and assessment process. The projects are collaborations among county offices of education, school districts, and institutes of higher education. Several of these collaborations are: (a) St. Mary's College, Contra Costa United School District, and Alameda County; (b) Cal State at Hayward, Oakland United School District, and Alameda County; and (c) Simpson College, Chico State, and Tehama County.

• The National Urban Alliance for Effective Education at Teachers College, Columbia University, will use the professional development portfolio with 50 K–12 teachers participating in a three-year staff development program aimed at "Thinking Across the Curriculum."

• In Contra Costa County, California, the assistant superintendent of curriculum and instruction organized a cluster of pilot groups from school districts across the county. The Contra Costa County Office is now sponsoring a network of professional development portfolio users. The county office began this network of districts by inviting school districts to send teams of administrators and teachers to learn and practice the process together. The first year has just been completed and there is a great deal of energy for continuing the network.

• The New York City school system in fall 1994 began a one-year pilot group with 25 teachers at five school sites using the professional development portfolio. During the pilot year, the implementation team will focus on building capacity to support the portfolio process. The building administrators as well as the teacher center staff have become familiar with the professional development portfolio process and have designed an implementation plan that includes evaluating the process during the year. Learnings from the pilot year will be reflected in adaptations to the process as they prepare to offer the portfolio as an option to teachers throughout the city in 1995.

IMPLICATIONS FOR STAFF DEVELOPERS
Schools that are ready to make a commitment to professional development for teachers that extend beyond the usual training sessions seem to find that the professional development portfolio enhances and extends their professional development efforts with teachers.

As we incorporate changes from the "portfolio pioneers," our attention turns to [the] next steps. We are eager to bring the professional development portfolio to other sites and to be part of positive actions for future-focused change. Creating a learning environment for *all* must begin with the staff ("you cannot give away what you do not have"). Our initial studies reveal that the portfolio process is indeed successful in helping school leadership become architects of learning environments for all and for staff development to be truly learner centered.

REFERENCES

Brooks, M., & Grennon-Brooks, J. (1987). Becoming a teacher of thinking: Constructivism, change, and consequence. *Journal of Staff Development*, 8(3), 23–27.

Dietz, M. E. (1993). *Change facilitation*. California affiliate of the National Staff Development Council.

———. (1994). *Professional development portfolio*. Boston: Sundance.

Gardner, H. (1991). *The unschooled mind*. New York: Basic Books.

Glasser, W. (1993). *The quality school teacher*. New York: Harper.

Joyce, B. (1990). *Changing school culture through staff development*. Alexandria, VA: Association for Supervision and Curriculum Development.

Krupp, J. A. (1987). *Understanding and motivating personnel in the second half of life*. Presented at the annual meeting of [the] American Educational Research Association, San Francisco.

Portfolio Assessment of Teachers

by Peggy G. Perkins and Jeffrey I. Gelfer

Evaluating teacher performance for improvement is a valuable way to enhance the quality of elementary and secondary school programs (Decker and Decker 1988). Each school program should organize its own criteria for evaluating teacher performance. In establishing the criteria, the principal should consider the philosophy and policies of the program, the roles and responsibilities of the teachers, and the qualities constituting effective and successful performance.

One of the general principles of evaluation is that it should be an ongoing process (Gronlund and Linn 1990). A continuous process can provide information

1. on how well the philosophy and goals of the program are being achieved;

2. about the effectiveness of each person on the staff;

3. about each one's knowledge of methods and materials; and

4. about personal attributes, enthusiasm, poise, and ability to adjust to frustrations, cooperate with colleagues, and accept constructive criticism.

It will also provide information to individuals on the staff about their job performance.

It is important for principals of secondary programs to be aware that both subjective data—which are dependent on the evaluator's feelings, opinions, and attitudes—and objective information are useful. Evaluations made by principals should be

From *The Clearing House,* vol. 66, no. 4. March–April 1993, pp. 235–37.
Reprinted with permission of the Helen Dwight Reid Educational Foundation.
Published by Heldref Publications, 1319 Eighteenth Street NW, Washington,
DC 20036-1802. Copyright © 1993.

informed, rational, and as insightful as possible. It is important that evaluation information be both relevant and accurate.

FEEDBACK AN IMPORTANT COMPONENT

Immediate feedback and access to recorded evaluation of performance have been found to be helpful and meaningful (Decker and Decker 1988), including exchanges between principal and faculty, and faculty and faculty. A teacher portfolio permits immediate feedback and allows for the process of evaluation to be continuous. The Joint Committee on Standards for Educational Evaluation (1981) identified four attributes that are essential for sound educational evaluation: utility, feasibility, propriety, and accuracy. These important standards can also be served by the portfolio approach. Portfolios for students have been found to be very helpful for organization, instructional development, student performance, and evaluation of students and the program (Flood and Lapp 1989; Jongsman 1989). A portfolio is a folder of personal data on an individual. The folder can include a record of achievement, samples of work, observations made by a supervisor, a colleague, or oneself, personal evaluations, and any other relevant data. Portfolios can help strengthen a faculty member's overall organization, demonstrate progress and innovative work, and provide information that helps improve performance and the quality of the overall program.

> A teacher portfolio permits immediate feedback and allows for the process of evaluation to be continuous.

Portfolios have commonly been used by professionals such as writers, actors, artists, and university educators. Artists rely on portfolios to demonstrate their skills, achievement, and creativity (Valencia 1990). Portfolios can provide artists with new insights, greater precision and techniques, new organizational skills, new interests, and valuable analysis of their growth and development. University educators have used portfolios to demonstrate their teaching performance and help obtain promotion.

THE TEACHER PORTFOLIO

Developing and implementing a teacher portfolio program requires planning, time, patience, organization, and cooperation from students, teachers, and principals. Before developing a teacher portfolio it would be helpful to examine the following questions:

1. What does a teacher portfolio look like?
2. How is it organized?
3. What are its contents?
4. What selection process should determine the portfolio's contents?
5. How will the teacher portfolio be evaluated?

The teacher portfolio can be an expandable file that includes samples of an individual faculty member's work, documenting his or her performance and professional growth over a period of time. A portfolio might be organized to include the following distinct sections:

- Planning
- Organization of instruction
- Presentation of knowledge
- Teacher-student interaction
- Teacher-parent relationships
- Assessment and evaluation
- Classroom management
- Curriculum development
- Professionalism

Teacher portfolios represent the teacher's management, creativity, organization, and effectiveness. Each staff member should select samples of daily work experiences to put in the portfolio. The contents may include observations made by [the] principal and faculty, written lesson plans, written progress reports, and slides and samples of bulletin boards and innovative projects. There might be samples of written communications distributed to parents, records of parent-teacher conferences, letters of appreciation from parents, or teacher performance checklists filled out by the principal. The portfolio might even include tape recordings and videos of lessons or special events during the school day. Other contents could be individual conference reports with the principal, records of workshops and educational training attended, and self-assessments.

Portfolios provide opportunities for teachers to select material that they perceive to reflect their best work. Staff thus become part of the evaluation process and focus their attention on how their work has changed.

SELECTION PROCESS

Teachers need to establish a system for deciding what should go into the portfolio during the school year. They could choose material that documents efficacy in areas such as the following:

- Knowledge of content and curriculum
- Providing appropriate learning experiences for students
- Appropriate planning
- Management of the environment and students' behaviors
- Human relationship and communication skills
- Recording and evaluating students' progress
- Use of available resources
- Fulfillment of professional responsibilities

Each week, faculty members should select the best representations of their work and productivity. Each month, they can remove contents that seem redundant or not representative of their performance. At the end of the year, they should be able to meet the competencies required by the principal and reflect upon their growth and progress, as well as their students' growth and progress.

EVALUATING THE PORTFOLIOS

Teacher portfolios can be evaluated on professional growth demonstrated by each individual as documented by his or her portfolio. A checklist of the competencies expected to be accomplished can be discussed at the beginning of the year (figure 1). Portfolios are to be reviewed by the principal and teachers throughout the year. Both contribute to the evaluation process. Portfolios allow teachers to evaluate their own performance, as well as contribute data that are helpful for the administration in determining staff growth and development. Evalua-

Figure 1
Samples of Expected Teacher Competencies

Content and Curriculum Coverage
- Activities promote problem solving, decision making, and creativity.
- Lessons are related to children's experiences.

Methodology and Classroom Organization
- Small groups in the classroom are flexible and related to the needs and interests of different students.
- Students are given opportunities to explore issues and concepts.

Planning
- Objectives are stated.
- Materials and equipment are listed.

Manages Classroom Instruction and Behavior
- Activities and teacher questions are sufficiently open-ended to allow creative and divergent thinking to occur.
- Teacher has established a set of rules and procedures to prevent disruptive behavior.

Communicates Effectively
- Teacher is sensitive to the needs and concerns of others.
- Teacher respects the rights of others.

Evaluates Students' Performance
- Teacher uses a variety of assessment and evaluation procedures.
- Teacher reports progress to parents.

Uses Appropriate Resources
- Media selections match learner variables.

Exhibits Professionalism
- Accepts constructive criticism and is willing to admit mistakes.
- Teacher is dedicated and enthusiastic.

Note: Levels of competencies can be indicated by designated code. For example, *S* represents satisfactory and *N* represents needs improvement.

tions of teacher performance, using portfolios, can be conducted once every school quarter or as often as the principal
believes is necessary.

   Using portfolios to help measure teacher growth and
development may build confidence, commitment, and enthusiasm among the faculty. Portfolios provides a lucid picture—for
both principal and teacher—of how staff members are developing and improving. They are a means to enhance working
attitudes and improve the quality of the program.

REFERENCES

Decker, C. A., and J. R. Decker. 1988. *Planning and administering early childhood programs.* Columbus, Ohio: Merrill Publishing.

Flood, J., and D. Lapp. 1989. Reporting reading progress: A comparison portfolio for parents. *The Reading Teacher* 1: 508–14.

Gronlund, N. E., and R. L. Linn. 1990. *Measurement and evaluation in teaching.* 6th ed. New York: Macmillan.

The Joint Committee on Standards for Educational Evaluation. 1981. *Standards for evaluation of educational programs, projects and materials.* New
   York: McGraw-Hill.

Jongsman, K. S. 1989. Portfolio assessment. *The Reading Teacher* 1: 264–65.

Valencia, S. V. 1990. A portfolio approach to classroom reading and assessment: The whys, whats and hows. *The Reading Teacher* 43(4): 338–40.

Scholarship Reconsidered: A Challenge to Use Teaching Portfolios to Document the Scholarship of Teaching

by Don M. Boileau

Perhaps no one more than Ernest L. Boyer has influenced decisions on the retention, promotion, and tenure of professors in this generation. *Scholarship Reconsidered: Priorities of the Professoriate,* sponsored by the Carnegie Foundation for the Advancement of Teaching, raised the essential issues for broadening the consideration of scholarship. Russell Edgerton, the President of the American Association of Higher Education, viewed the report as "…reclaiming the common ground of scholarship that underlies" teaching, service, and research. The former President of Stanford University, Donald Kennedy, saw the report as dispelling the polarity between teaching and scholarship as a way to achieve "a more rigorous and healthy version of the academy—and importantly, for a renewal and revitalization of teaching as well." Derek Bok, former president of Harvard University, believed that *Scholarship Reconsidered* [s]poke directly to the renewed debate ". . . over the faculty's preoccupation with research and its effects on the quality of teaching." (The Edgerton, Kennedy and Bok quotations are from promotional literature of the Carnegie Foundation.)

In another vein, Peter Seldin's *Successful Use of Teaching Portfolios* awakens the professoriate to ways to enhance the conversation among peers as to teaching. Seldin observed how

Boyer's work created the new emphasis on teaching by national emphasis on ". . . the insistent viewpoint that teaching is actually an expression of scholarship, that scholarship does not confine itself to the cutting edge of research, but also lives in intimate knowledge and teaching of the research in the classroom."

From these two contributions communication departments gain immensely by having rationales and a vocabulary to present to our colleagues in other disciplines and sciences about the work we do. Our Greek heritage created rhetoric as a useful art that enhanced the quality of public life—the study of rhetoric was essential to a democratic society. While the necessity of communication studies in the academy is obvious to most of us, we are also familiar with the difficulty that some colleagues have had with other faculty about the seriousness of scholarship for those faculty engaged in debate/forensics, directing productions on the stage or in the studio, producing videos, researching communication in organizational settings, studying communication in the classroom, etc. Boyer's schemata provide us with a structure and vocabulary for promoting these activities within the scholarship rubric. Within the scholarship of teaching, the portfolio method also allows us to expand the structure and vocabulary for the evaluation and improvement of teaching.

> The portfolio method allows us to expand the structure and vocabulary for the evaluation and improvement of teaching.

THE CONTEXT: *SCHOLARSHIP RECONSIDERED*'S CONTRIBUTIONS

Boyer argues simply that we need to change the definition of the work of faculty "in ways that reflect more realistically the full range of academic and civic mandates" (p. 16). In essence the book argues to change the traditional reliance on research and publication as the only measures of a faculty. Harvard's President Bok observed, "Collectively, however, faculties often seem distressingly sluggish and unwilling to change" (1986, p. 184). After documenting the dissatisfaction among college faculties about the present system, Boyer provides a rhetorical answer in keeping the word "scholarship" in four phrases to describe faculty activity. To do this the book argues for four separate, yet overlapping functions.

Closest to what academics speak of as traditional research is the concept **scholarship of discovery,** which is the discovery of new knowledge by "disciplined, investigative efforts within the academy" (p. 17). The outcomes, the process, and the passion of original research define this category.

Also valuable is **the scholarship of integration,** by which Boyer means "…making connections across the disciplines, placing the specialties in larger context, illuminating data in a revealing way, often educating nonspecialist too" (p. 18). These ideas come from "disciplined work that seeks to interpret, draw together, and bring new insight to bear on original research." Kenneth Anderson's classic article on ethos is this type of work. Boyer notes:

> The distinction we are drawing here between "discovery" and "integration" can be best understood, perhaps, by the questions posed. Those engaged in discovery ask, "What is to be known, what is yet to be found?" Those engaged in integration ask, "What do the findings mean? Is it possible to interpret what's been discovered in ways that provide a larger, more comprehensive understanding?" (p. 19).

The writer is looking for patterns that connect and, as such, often is working at interdisciplinary boundaries. The connection between knowledge and audience is not only a communicative concern but one based on the desire to help others understand what people have added to the field of the known. Societal problems often demand integration of knowledge. The former president of the University of Hawaii, Harlan Cleveland, noted:

> The academy's students, and its outside critics too, notice that the vertical academic disciplines, built around clusters of related methodologies, are not in themselves very helpful in solving problems. No real world problem can be fitted into the jurisdiction of a single academic department (1974, p. 13).

The third area, **the scholarship of application,** explores those areas in which the scholar asks, "How can knowledge be responsibly applied to consequential problems? How can it be helpful to individuals as well as institutions?" (p. 22). Here a distinction must be drawn between those activities of citizenship within the civic and academic communities and those activities that relate to "one's special field of knowledge and relate to, and flow directly out of, this professional activity" (p. 22). Work in this area often responds to those areas where problems of society define the needs and vagaries of action. A work like [that of] Mark Hickson and Don Stacks (1992), *Effective Communication for Academic Chairs,* meets this standard as knowledge of the communication discipline is applied in each of those article[s] to the needs of academic chairs. It is a service for all chairs in providing approaches to overcoming the challenges of being a department chair.

> **These four forms of scholarship form an interdependent whole in ways that allow us to expand the narrowness of "publish or perish."**

The last area is the important area of **the scholarship of teaching,** which deals with those areas in which the transmitting, transformation, and extension of knowledge occurs. This area moves between the vitality of changing the classroom to promote better learning to the development of pedagogical writings. "Great teachers create a common ground of intellectual commitment . . . and encourage students to be critical, creative thinkers" (p. 24). The base of such activity comes from knowing as "Those who teach must, above all be well informed, and steeped in the knowledge of their fields. Teaching can be well regarded only as professors are widely read and intellectually engaged" (p. 23). The thoughtful educator Parker Palmer in his (1993) American Association of Higher Education keynote address remarked about the distinctiveness of teaching as part of a unique community of higher education—one that does not reflect the therapeutic, civic, or business communities. For him this scholarship of teaching is inherent in the research we do, not in a dichotomy of doing one or the other, but in the way that our research informs and develops our teaching.

Essential to Boyer's view is that these four forms of scholarship form an interdependent whole in ways that allow us to expand the narrowness of "publish or perish" with its corollary that true scholarship is research. It prevents the narrowness of claiming that textbooks or articles in the *Journal of Applied Communication* are not suitable for consideration of tenure and promotion (Boyer, p. 35). This expanded view of contributions by scholarship still leave[s] us with the valuative question about what is excellence, what is a national reputation, and/or what has advanced the field. In these questions one discovers the contributions of thoughtful scholarship.

It is not that these contributions should not be evaluated rigorously, but that scholarship of any type "...can reveal a professor's knowledge of the field, illuminate essential integrative themes, and powerfully contribute to excellence in teaching" (p. 35). The challenge becomes how to take these concerns to go beyond the usual ranking of research publications to measure scholarship. In the 1989 Carnegie Foundation national survey of faculty some 68 percent agreed [with] the statement that "at my institution we need better ways, besides publications, to evaluate the scholarly performance of the faculty" (Boyer, p. 34). (Note that the community colleges had the lowest rate of agreement at 55 percent while the comprehensive university had the highest at 80 percent.)

Given this major problem facing faculty, of how do we evaluate these other forms of teaching—the realistic question created by *Scholarship Reconsidered*—one must consider the efforts of the American Association of Higher Education (AAHE) to move teaching evaluation beyond the usual student opinion ratings as some type of systematic, just system for the area of the scholarship of teaching. The teaching portfolio movement has the similar impact as Boyer's work in expanding the horizons of those interested in the evaluation of teaching.

TEACHING PORTFOLIOS PROMOTE THE SCHOLARSHIP OF TEACHING

At most institutions, lip service is paid to teaching by the use of student evaluations. At my own institution, six university level questions are used for all faculty, while the departments and individuals can add their own for individual purposes. The last provost urged that departments add their own observation systems and an analysis of syllabi. Last year, the provost's office, on the recommendation of the University Life Committee, held a convocation to consider the use of portfolios as a way to improve teaching and to give faculty the option of using them as part of the record for establishing judgments about effective teaching.

Definition

The Portfolio Movement serves as a way to document teaching efforts by taking advantage of (a) reflective thinking on one's teaching; (b) sharing of what one does with a mentor or colleague as a way to create a dialogue on teaching; and (c) the creation of dialogue on campus about teaching as a way to end the privatization of teaching.

Portfolios are generally three-ring binders that create teaching records including most often three types of materials:

1. Products of Good Teaching (examples of graded essays along with comments, students' publications or other student work, statements by alumni on the quality of work);

2. Material from Oneself (a reflective statement describing one's personal teaching philosophy, strategies, and objectives, statement of teaching responsibilities, representative syllabi, description of curricular revisions, steps taken to improve teaching, creative assignments and tests); and

3. Materials from Others (observation reports on one's teaching, student course and teaching evaluation data, teaching award information, invitations to present ideas on teaching at conferences, statements from colleagues who have reviewed the teaching materials of the course).

Functions

Portfolios increase the dialogue on teaching by helping to create "conversations" with:

(a)   *A mentor and/or colleague.* Often a mentor from another discipline will be forced to ask "WHY?" more often, not knowing the links within the discipline, while the colleague from the discipline helps with content;

(b)   *An evaluation committee.* The portfolio switches the measurement of teaching from data points to a wide range of teaching activities and measurements. A better gestalt of teaching is created; and

(c) *Evidence of teaching for job searches.* The portfolio serves as evidence of teaching that committees can examine during hiring processes. Universities should be asking for evidence of teaching effectiveness—the portfolio is becoming a nationally acceptable way of documenting teaching activity.

While this paper is more concerned with the first two functions of increasing dialogue about teaching as a way to legitimize teaching conversations and evaluation, the third function flows from the others and is one that administrators should consider as part of the evaluation of candidates. Portfolios definitely are a way to provide *evidence of teaching effectiveness* by the candidates.

> **Portfolios definitely are a way to provide *evidence of teaching effectiveness* by the candidates.**

The major contribution most advocates of portfolios mention is the *perceived improvement of teaching.* Portfolios increase reflection and action about teaching by:

(a) giving focus on teaching as part of a professor's expected activities;

(b) encouraging faculty to seek ways to improve their teaching by attending conference meetings on teaching, reading about teaching techniques, and creating discussions about teaching within the department and university; and

(c) stimulating formal and informal research on teaching.

As someone having to evaluate faculty constantly on teaching, the idea of expanding items to include for the scholarship of teaching is enticing. Among the 49 items listed by Edgerton, et al. (1991, p. 8) that relate specifically to our discipline are:

1. "Publications by students on course-related work"—could be papers at student panels at conventions; papers at several of the national honors conferences for students; forensic speeches in communication analysis; videos done in competitions.

2. "Setting up or running a successful internship"—a common feature of most of our departments, but definitely a way to look at a different type of teaching activity.

3. "Meetings intended to improve teaching"—the many basic course workshops, short courses at SCA and the regional, summer conferences, e.g., the small college series at Hope College, the C-SPAN workshops, are ways to enhance this standard.

4. "A media interview on a successful teaching innovation"—many of the activities in our classes would qualify as the normal procedures for group work and class debates often draw upon the expertise of our field; the SCA and ECA series on "Teachers on Teaching" provides evidence of national recognition of teaching skill.

The other 45 items have a generic quality to them. No matter what form it is in, this expanded vision of what EVIDENCE one can provide acknowledges teaching activity. A lot of detail can be added, but my purpose in this article is to link portfolios to the consideration of the scholarship of teaching. Both ideas not only help the profession in general, but also help our discipline expand the ways to document what we do to help students learn.

REFERENCES AND NOTES

Bok, D. (1986). *Higher Education*. Cambridge, MA: Harvard University Press.

Boyer, E. L. (1990). *Scholarship Reconsidered: Priorities of the Professoriate*. Princeton, NJ: The Carnegie Foundation for the Advancement of Teaching.

Cleveland, H. (January, 1974). Seven Everyday Collisions in American Higher Education (Occasional Paper #9). International Council for Educational Development.

Edgerton, R., Hutchins, P., & Quinlan, K. (1991). *The Teaching Portfolio: Capturing the Scholarship in Teaching*. Washington, DC: American Association for Higher Education.

Hickson, M., & Stacks, D. W. (1992). *Effective Communication for Academic Chairs*. Albany, NY: State University of New York Press.

Seldin, P., and Associates. (1993). *Successful Use of Teaching Portfolios*. Bolton, MA: Anker Publishing Company.

This article is based upon a paper presentation at the Eastern Communication Association Convention on April 29, 1993, in New Haven, CT.

Performance Evaluation Journey: The Summative Plan

Portfolios, when used for assessing teacher performance, are a new approach compared to the more traditional ones, especially classroom observations. They can be a valuable addition as a source of evidence on teaching performance.—Patricia Wheeler

The formative professional portfolios reviewed in section two are what some have called "low-stakes" portfolios. They are being used by several states, educational agencies, teacher education programs, and school districts primarily for preservice training, self-evaluation, and professional development for the purpose of improving classroom teaching and learning. However, another type of portfolio, the "high-stakes" or summative portfolio, is being developed and/or used for assessing teacher performance and evaluating individuals "in order to make decisions about successful program completion, licensure, hiring and job assignments, and other personnel decisions" (Wheeler).

These summative portfolios usually delineate not only what items need to be included to show accountability but also how the final product will be evaluated. Many groups are still struggling with developing reliable rubrics, or scoring guides, since the scoring is heavily dependent on the professional judgment of those doing the evaluating. These so-called high-stakes portfolios require that those doing the scoring, as well as the participants, know in advance the performance criteria, scoring rubrics, benchmarks, and ratings guidelines that will be used in the final evaluation. After all, people's grades, licenses, promotions, or jobs could be at stake.

Patricia Wheeler, in her article "Using Portfolios to Assess Teacher Performance," suggests that schools begin the assessment process by asking teachers to create portfolios for professional development and for encouraging teacher self-evaluation and reflection. However, if the schools decide to use portfolios as part of the teacher evaluation process, Wheeler believes they should "proceed with caution." She recommends experimenting first with what is feasible to include, as well as understanding "teacher performance in various job assignments and school contexts" to allow for more accurate and meaningful scoring.

Estelle Gellman discusses the question of the validity of portfolio evaluation, "the question of whether a measurement instrument is, in fact, assessing that which we want to assess," in her article "The Use of Portfolios in Assessing Teacher Competence: Measurement Issues." She finds that even though portfolios are very individualistic in their contents, they can be prepared to respond to a standard task or set of tasks. According to Gellman, an acceptable level of reliability can be obtained "if there is a common set of criteria on which to judge this set of products, and if there is adequate inter-rater reliability in the judgments of the raters."

In his article "The Schoolteacher's Portfolio: Issues in Design, Implementation, and Evaluation," Kenneth Wolf describes the evaluation procedures used in the Teacher Assessment Project (TAP) at Stanford, in which evaluators used a draft of the standards from the National Board for Professional Teaching Standards. In the Stanford project, examiners who were experienced and knowledgeable in the applicable content and grade level were trained to rate each portfolio according to the broad criteria established by the national board. Wolf reports that, "in scoring the portfolios, each entry, as well as the candidate's overall performance, was rated for each appropriate standard on a five-point scale: unacceptable, weak, adequate, proficient, and superb." And while he agrees that many forms of teacher evaluation are fundamentally flawed, Wolf adds that "portfolios are flawed as well, but no other method of assessment can equal them in providing a connection to the contexts and personal histories of real teaching."

Christine Hult, in her article "Using Portfolios to Assess Teachers: Learning from Ourselves," expresses her concern about the confusion in purposes when assessing teachers. She asks, "What are our reasons for evaluating teachers anyway? What do we hope to accomplish? Two related but conflicting goals underlie most teacher evaluation: one is the goal of accountability (achieved through summative evaluations of performance); the other is the goal of improvement in classroom teaching and learning (achieved through formative evaluations of performance). Too often in teacher evaluation, the two goals are conflated." While the more informal, formative portfolio emphasizes reflection and professional growth, the more formal, summative portfolio emphasizes accountability for the criteria, goals, or standards as measured by trained raters. School districts and teachers need to determine which type of portfolio best fits their purposes for using portfolios.

And finally, Helen Regan's article, "Integrated Portfolios as Tools for Differentiated Teacher Evaluation: A Proposal," offers a recommendation to reduce principal evaluations: have administrators perform different types of evaluations for novice and experienced teachers. She states, "For novice teachers, evaluations should emphasize accountability, but for experienced teachers whose fundamental competence has been established, evaluations should more properly emphasize professional development." Regan discusses her belief that current teacher-evaluation practices make unrealistic demands on administrators' time and suggests requiring one type of "comprehensive portfolio" that includes a narrative for evaluating novice teachers and another, shorter portfolio, called "critical incident portfolio," for veteran teachers.

The following articles provide insight into the differences between the professional development portfolio (formative) described in Section 2, which is used primarily for teacher reflection and self-assessment, and the professional portfolio (summative), which is used for both professional development and performance accountability. As Wheeler states,

> Portfolios can make a worthwhile contribution not only to the evaluation process, but also to the improvement of teaching and instruction for all students. Once they are accepted and teachers have some experience compiling them, portfolio use in professional development, assessment, and performance evaluation can be more fully implemented.

Using Portfolios to Assess Teacher Performance

by Patricia H. Wheeler

The collection of data and information to assess teachers' performance can be done through various avenues. These approaches may include observations, interviews, surrogate tasks, tests, questionnaires, rating forms, videotaping, and portfolios. A teacher evaluation system should have more than one way to collect data and should rely on more than one source of data (e.g., observations by peers, ratings by students and parents, interviews by principals). Portfolios have gained much attention in recent years for the assessment of both teacher performance and student learning. What is not often recognized is that portfolios have been used for many years. As Bird (1990) points out, "the schoolteacher's portfolio would not be as interesting if it were called 'the teacher personnel file.'" This is also true for student folders, a method by which teachers monitor student learning and development.

What then is a teacher portfolio? What it isn't is an instrument to gather data and information, such as a test or a rating form. It isn't simply a repository for, or a collection of, materials. A *portfolio* is a purposeful collection of selected materials by and/or about the teacher.

Teacher portfolios are being used by several states, educational agencies, teacher education programs, and school districts, usually for low-stake purposes such as preservice training, self-evaluation, and professional development. While many agencies are still in the exploratory or field-testing phase (e.g., professional certification of experienced teachers by the Na-

From *EREAPA Publication Series,* no. 93–7, 1993, ED 364 967. © 1993 by Patricia H. Wheeler. Reprinted with permission.

tional Board for Professional Teaching Standards, beginning teacher licensure in Connecticut, the master teacher program in Texas), some agencies are now using portfolios for assessing performance and evaluating individuals in order to make decisions about successful program completion, licensure, hiring and job assignments, and other personnel decisions (e.g., career ladder programs in Arizona and Tennessee, teacher licensure in Oregon).

> Portfolios, as well as other approaches to collecting data and information, can serve many *purposes.*

KEY POLICY DECISIONS

The structure of a portfolio, its contents, and the use of materials in it are determined by key policy decisions that should be addressed prior to its preparation by teachers. These include:

1. the purposes of the assessment and the evaluation;
2. the domains to be covered, at least in part, by the portfolios;
3. the audience who will use the portfolios;
4. the individuals who will compile and update the portfolios;
5. the individuals who will have access to the portfolios;
6. the procedures to be used to protect the materials and the confidentiality of information in and about the portfolio;
7. the individuals who will retain the portfolios, where and for how long;
8. the types of materials to be included in the portfolio;
9. technical issues; and
10. legal issues.

Portfolios, as well as other approaches to collecting data and information, can serve many *purposes.* At the school level, they can be used for personnel decision making, program and school improvement and evaluation efforts, staff development programs, and as a source of models and ideas for teachers. A teacher can use his/her portfolio for professional development, reflection, and self-evaluation. An individual, whether currently employed as a teacher or not, can use a portfolio for job seeking, obtaining awards, professional certification, self-evaluation, professional fulfillment, and documenting his/her own career history. When used for development or for formative evaluation, portfolios are often called "working portfolios"; when used for high-stakes decisions, such as hiring or licensing, or for summative evaluations, they are sometimes called "presentation portfolios." Some of these purposes are low-stake ones, but others may have high stakes associated with them. The issue of whether portfolio preparation is a solo or a coached process also needs to be addressed, and is discussed more under "Guidelines for Compiling the Portfolio."

> **The *audience* for the portfolios will determine what materials are to be included.**

Domains are those broad areas covering an array of teaching behaviors reflected in the performance criteria of the evaluation system. For instance, the domains in the duties-of-the-teacher list include: Knowledge of the Subject Matter, Instructional Skills, Assessment Skills, Professionalism, and Other Services to the School (Scriven, 1991). Although materials in portfolios can apply to any of these five domains (see below), some domains, or elements within the domains (e.g., Management of Process Skills under the domain of Instructional Skills), are better assessed by other means. Shulman (1988) points out that no one approach to assessing teacher performance can cover all domains adequately. The use of portfolios in conjunction with other approaches (e.g., observations, interviews, student ratings) can provide more comprehensive information for use in determining a teacher's level of performance.

The *audience* for the portfolios will determine what materials are to be included. If it is being used primarily by those persons providing professional development and support to the teacher, similar types of materials gathered over extended periods of time should be included. This permits assessment of progress over time on similar attributes of teaching. If the portfolio is to be used by professional certification boards or by administrators for promotion decisions, it will probably include examples of the teacher's best work, since the teacher wishes to demonstrate a high level of performance worthy of special recognition. If the portfolio is going to be used by an evaluator for annual performance reviews, it should include examples of typical work, randomly collected across the school year. This will provide a more comprehensive picture of the performance level of the teacher and whether that level improves or declines over the school year and across school years. It also allows the evaluator to determine if the teacher is adapting and adopting practices to better address the needs of the students and, if student-produced artifacts are included in the teacher's portfolio, whether or not students are making progress toward the curricular goals and instructional objectives. When used in an interview or conference as part of the evaluation process, a portfolio having typical materials from across the school year provides opportunities to question changes in practice and reflect on performance over the full year and across years.

> The *types of materials to be included* in the portfolio should probably be given the most thought.

The next four decisions are concerned with *administrative matters.* These issues should be addressed early in the process so that teachers who are compiling portfolios have no surprises at a later date, better understand their responsibilities with regard to preparing portfolios, and have a clearer understanding of who will have access to their portfolio materials and how they will use the portfolios.

These are not easy policy issues to contemplate and must be considered in terms of the entire teacher evaluation policy for the school or district. However, number 8 on the list above—the *types of materials to be included* in the portfolio—should probably be given the most thought. Numerous possibilities exist including student work, reflective essays by the teacher, and teacher-produced instructional activities. (More examples are in the next section.) Portfolios may become overwhelmingly large and time-consuming for both teachers and evaluators if some limitation is not placed on the types of materials to be included.

Technical issues need to be addressed with any approach for assessing teacher performance, including portfolios. These include relevance to the job of teaching, comparability across teaching assignments and contexts, accuracy and consistency of the scoring process, use of appropriate scoring scales for the intended purpose, reasonable and justifiable interpretations of results, the use of portfolio data in conjunction with other assessment data and information, the combining of portfolio results with other assessment results, and the setting of standards for acceptable performance.

Legal issues include protecting the confidentiality of the teacher and others including the students, ensuring authenticity of the items in the portfolio, addressing the potential for cheating and plagiarism, establishing or providing for appeals processes, complying with union agreements, and protecting against misuse of the results, as well as damage to or loss of any items in the portfolio while not in the possession of the teacher.

DESIGN OF PORTFOLIOS

After these policy decisions have been made, the guidelines for compiling the portfolio, what specific materials are to be included, and how the materials will be scored or evaluated should be determined.

Guidelines for Compiling the Portfolio

Features of the portfolios may include: designation of materials to be included; whether the process of compiling the portfolio is a solo or a coached effort; whether it is a one-time or an ongoing effort; whether it represents best, typical, or developmental performance; and what development, assessment, and evaluation processes are to be used in conjunction with the portfolios.

Portfolio compilation procedures can be very specific about what materials are to be included. Some fanciful examples may be: a list of instructional activities for the third period of the second Tuesday in November, the first teacher-made test given in January, an essay written by the teacher during the first week of December reflecting on classroom management strategies used the fourth day of school and six weeks later, samples of the homework assignment completed by three students whose names start with or follow "Det" on the alphabetic roster, and a list of all training sessions attended through spring vacation. Or it could be left entirely up to the teacher to decide what to include. It could also be a mixture of specified and unspecified materials.

The materials collected in the portfolio can reflect more than teaching performance. Just as some teachers are good actors when an observer is present, or are able to talk their way through any situation in an interview, some individuals can compile impressive materials to market themselves as outstanding teachers. Is it fair to a teacher who doesn't have such skills to be judged in the same manner as one who can do a great marketing job through a portfolio? If the portfolio is to be a valid representation of a teacher's performance rather than his/her marketing skills, it makes sense for a certain amount of coaching to be provided to all teachers, especially in the early stages of compiling portfolios. As Shulman (1988, 1991) points out, graduate students are coached through their doctoral dissertations, though the student is ultimately responsible for the final product and mastery of the subject area. The same should be done for teachers preparing portfolios and, as part of the evaluation process, teachers should be asked to explain or clarify items in the portfolio. This may be done in an individual interview and/or in a group setting, such as a staff meeting or a professional development activity.

> **Procedures and policies should be established so that the portfolio materials reflect the type of performance being assessed.**

A portfolio takes a significant amount of time to compile. To stop activities to compile one could be quite disruptive to the instructional process. If teachers are collecting materials over time, they should receive regular reminders to this effect, especially for developmental portfolios. Otherwise large blocks of time (i.e., several weeks or months) might not be represented or possibly only represented by materials prepared long after the event to which they refer took place, increasing the possibility of inaccuracies and omissions. To minimize disruptions to instruction and to improve the accuracy and comprehensiveness of materials and information, the portfolio compilation should be an ongoing process throughout the year.

When being very specific about what materials are to be included (see example above), teachers may put too much effort into those products, thus representing best efforts rather than typical ones. Procedures and policies should be established so that the portfolio materials reflect the type of performance being assessed (i.e., developmental, typical, best). Wolf (1991a) asks, "Should the schoolteacher's portfolio resemble the photographer's, which presents only the very best work, or the pilot's log, in which every flight is recorded? Should the portfolio display all of a person's work—the good, the bad, and the ugly—or only the work of which the person is most proud?" (p. 134).

Portfolios are most helpful when used with other development, assessment, and evaluation processes. Such uses should be identified in the guidelines for compiling the portfolios, and procedures should be given to meet the other uses. These include: meeting the schedules and deadlines for collecting certain materials so that they will be available for use in other assessments, including materials that cover the same lessons or units as other assessments so as to provide a common basis for interpreting the various assessment results, including those materials in the portfolio that will be used to provide background for an observation or as stimulus items for an interview, and including materials related to areas of weakness being addressed by a teacher's plan of professional improvement.

Specific Materials to Be Included
Criteria for determining which specific items to include in portfolios are:

1. the relevance to the performance criteria and domains addressed by the assessment and evaluation system;

2. the use of materials for which authenticity can be ensured;

3. the reliability of the materials as a source of evidence about the teacher's level of performance;

4. the usefulness for substantiating or supporting other sources of assessment data;

5. the use of the item in other aspects of professional development, assessment, and evaluation processes (e.g., prompts for interviews, examples to track progress in a teaching skill);

6. the provision of important evidence that cannot be obtained readily or accurately through other assessment instruments or processes;

7. the elimination of unnecessary duplication of other

assessment approaches and data sources;

    8. the added value of each item to other information in the portfolio;

    9. the time, cost, and other resources required to produce or obtain the item;

    10. the feasibility of judging the quality of the materials; and

    11. the protection of confidentiality of data about other individuals.

The portfolio collection must be more concerned with quality and usefulness in the assessment process than with quantity. Materials should be authentic in their portrayal of the teacher's level of performance, and lend themselves to accurate and reliable scoring procedures. Evaluators must be able to make sound judgments, using carefully developed scoring rubrics and performance stand-ards, about a teacher's performance based on the items in the portfolio.

> **Evaluators must be able to make sound judgments about a teacher's performance based on the items in the portfolio.**

Portfolios can easily get out of hand and become costly, time-consuming, and a useless exercise of collecting and storing. The value of additional items for judging teaching per-formance diminishes as the number of such items increases, es-pecially if the items are similar. For example, one is not apt to learn much more about a teacher's test-construction skills from four teacher-made tests than three of them, but can such per-formance be judged accurately by looking at only one teacher-made test? Usually not.

Some items that might be included in a portfolio for each of the five domains of the duties-based teacher evaluation sys-tem (Scriven, 1991) are provided in Table 1. These should not be regarded as comprehensive lists of what can be included, but rather as a source of initial ideas. Certainly a portfolio does not have to include this many items. It is important to be selective in what types and how many items are to be included. Portfolio compilation should not consume far more time than warranted and become a meaningless exercise.

Table 1
Examples of Items for Each of the Five Domains in the Duties-Based Teacher Evaluation System (Scriven, 1991) that Could Be Included in a Portfolio

Domain	Item
Knowledge of the Subject Matter	Reviews of two possible new textbooks A list of subject-related courses completed and workshops or conferences attended during the past year A reflective commentary on how to integrate art and science instruction
Instructional Skills	A list of instructional activities for a unit Statement of instructional goals and objectives for the year A reflective essay, written at the end of the first semester, on progress toward meeting the instructional goals and objectives Teacher's rationale for sequencing instructional topics Given a math problem, teacher provides three approaches to solving it Given a poem, teacher writes an essay on how different students might interpret it, given their backgrounds Videotape of the teacher presenting a lesson in the classroom A copy of the signed Standard First Aid training card from the Red Cross A list of those school and community sources of materials with which the teacher is familiar and which have been used in the past semester A log on the use of available technology by the teacher and by the students Photographs of three teacher-made displays used in instruction
Assessment Skills	Copies of two teacher-made unit tests or summaries of student assessment procedures A copy of the scoring rubrics used for a student project or report An essay describing the teacher's record-keeping system and how it is used to monitor student progress Samples of graded student work with comments from the teacher written on them Samples of the progress reports/letters sent to parents at the end of the first and third quarters
Professionalism	Record of participation in the school's professional development program activities this year Log of service, support to other teachers at the school this year Samples of written feedback to students of different backgrounds and ability levels to see if the feedback is fair and reasonable, given the ability level and background of each student Copies of any materials submitted to professional newsletters and journals Information on any awards received related to teaching (e.g., certificate, letter, newspaper article)
Other Services to the School	Copies of committee membership lists on which the teacher served this year List of after-school activities that the teacher supervised this year

Portfolio contents should include: (1) materials produced by the teacher (e.g., [a] list of instructional activities, reflective essays); (2) products of teaching (e.g., student work, videotapes of the classroom); and (3) information from others (e.g., letters from parents, copies of awards, committee lists). Materials may be linked to one lesson or unit (e.g., the list of activities and materials/equipment for each activity, a videotape of the lesson being implemented, three students' maps and reports, and a reflective essay, all on one geography activity) rather than different ones throughout the school year.

> [Portfolio] materials may be linked to one lesson or unit rather than different ones throughout the year.

Each item can provide evidence on multiple aspects of teaching. For example, the unit plan in the biology portfolios of the Teacher Assessment Project were reviewed for three types of evidence: instructional sequence, justification for including the topic in the syllabus, and a reasoned or descriptive reflection about the success or failure of the unit (Collins, 1990a). A teacher-made test can be used for evidence about assessment skills, knowledge of the subject area, and understanding of the students' test-taking skills.

Materials can be adapted for different teacher assignments. A mentor teacher might be asked to prepare a log of support provided to student teachers and new teachers, or a copy of the plan of assistance for a teacher coping with a group of disruptive students. A resource teacher might include an audio tape of a session working with a small group of students, or notes from a planning conference with another teacher. A special education teacher might include some individual education plans (IEPs), or a student progress report sent to the speech therapist.

The assessment procedures must delineate not only what items are to be included in a portfolio, but also how they will be scored for use in the professional development and/or evaluation of the teacher.

Scoring Process for Materials in Portfolios

When designing portfolios, it is important to address the scoring process issues. These include:

1. whether each piece, selected pieces, combinations of pieces, or the total collection will be scored;

2. whether analytic, holistic, or a combination of scoring approaches will be used;

3. who will do the scoring and what training they will receive;

4. what scoring rubrics will be used to judge or grade each item, and who will develop them and select and/or prepare the benchmarks to go with them;

5. who will monitor the judges and ensure the fairness, accuracy, and integrity of the scoring process; and

6. what type of scale or system will be used to report the results of the portfolio scoring to the individual teacher and to others (e.g., mentor teacher, evaluator).

Although many schools, districts, and teacher training institutions have started using portfolios, few have put extensive effort into developing solid scoring procedures. "The Stanford Teacher Assessment Project . . . found that the holistic approach allowed teaching to be examined in a more coherent fashion and avoided chopping up the act of teaching into many disconnected pieces" (Far West Lab, 1993, p. 33). Holistic scoring is usually less costly than analytic scoring. For overall performance evaluation, holistic scoring is probably more appropriate, whereas analytic scoring of selected items may be needed for professional development and self-evaluation purposes.

Scoring of portfolio materials is heavily dependent on the professional judgment of those doing the scoring. The need for clear performance criteria, scoring rubrics, benchmarks, and rating guidelines is critical. The selection of scorers must consider the degree of knowledge and experience needed with regard to the subject area, the types of students, and the school context. Thorough training and monitoring of scorers must be part of the portfolio assessment and evaluation processes.

The setting of standards is not part of the scoring process per se. The standards indicate what levels of performance or what scores are deemed acceptable for a given purpose. One can score a test, for example, but still not say if that score fulfills a requirement, such as passing a course. Standards should be set as part of the evaluation system's policy, rather than as part of the design for each assessment used in the evaluation process.

THE ADVANTAGES AND DISADVANTAGES OF USING PORTFOLIOS

There are advantages and disadvantages of using portfolios to assess and evaluate teachers. Several of these are discussed below.

Advantages of Using Portfolios

Edgerton, Hutchings, and Quinlan (1991) identify four reasons to use college teaching portfolios:

> First, portfolios can capture the intellectual substance and "situated-ness" of teaching in ways that other methods of evaluation cannot. Second, because of this capacity, portfolios encourage faculty to take important, new roles in the documentation, observation, and review of teaching. Third, because they prompt faculty to take these new roles, portfolios are a particularly powerful tool for improvement. Fourth, as more faculty come to use them, portfolios can help forge a new campus culture of professionalism about teaching. (p. 4)

In terms of using portfolios compared to other data collection approaches (e.g., observations, interviews, tests), portfolios can contain a variety of materials (as illustrated in Table 1), can reflect many of the tasks of teaching (in and out of the classroom), and can provide evidence for several domains.

Portfolios reflect the complexities of teaching and can provide flexibility and latitude for various types of teaching assignments. It is difficult to observe teachers who work with very small groups of students with special needs, or to observe resource teachers or short-term substitute teachers. It may not be feasible to observe teachers in very crowded classrooms or at off-site activities (e.g., field trips, music competitions, science fairs). Portfolios can be adapted to any type of teaching situation, especially if teachers are allowed to include items beyond what is specified for inclusion.

Portfolios can include evidence not readily available through other approaches. These may be letters from peers or parents, samples of students' work, awards, and copies of publications and products. They lend themselves to the collection of evidence from multiple sources (e.g., the teacher, students, peers, parents, supervisors, trainers, mentors, newspapers, project reports).

Portfolios encourage self-evaluation, reflection, self-improvement, and professional development. Bird points out that for new teachers, "a portfolio procedure could provide occasions to plan, monitor, support, and record the new teacher's attainments" (1990, p. 244). In their study in Ohio, Berry et al. (1991) found that keeping portfolios helped new teachers develop classroom management skills, content pedagogy, command of the subject matter, student specific pedagogy, and professional responsibilities. For both new and more experienced teachers, "A portfolio procedure could provide colleagues something concrete to admire, a discipline for assembling the evidence, an audience to admire it, and an occasion for doing so" (Bird, 1990, p. 245). Persons involved in the scoring of portfolios have an opportunity "for cultivating new and richer ways of thinking about and inquiring into the scholarship of teaching" (Edgerton et al., 1991, p. 6). It can be a professionally rewarding and enlightening experience (McRobbie, 1992).

> **Portfolios can increase the coverage of teacher behavior when used with other assessment methods.**

Portfolios, then, can increase the coverage of teacher behavior when used with other assessment methods. They can provide increased situational specificity for the setting or context within which the teacher is working. They can be tailored to different teaching assignments. Portfolio compilation provides opportunities for increased professional development, motivates teachers to improve, promotes self-evaluation, and increases the understanding of the teaching profession.

Disadvantages of Using Portfolios

Despite the many advantages of portfolios, there are also disadvantages, many related to the implementation of their use. "Portfolios are messy to construct, cumbersome to store, difficult to score, and vulnerable to misrepresentation" (Wolf, 1991a, p. 129). Some of these problems are more likely to occur in high-stakes evaluation programs than with low-stake uses such as self-evaluation and professional development.

In terms of portfolio content, some items may not be representative of the teacher's work, as specified in the evaluation procedures for selecting items to include. Although the procedures may call for typical items, teachers might put in their best examples or items that reflect most positively on them (e.g., sample work from the best students in the class, favorable letters from parents).

Compilation of an attractive portfolio can affect the scoring process. Some teachers know how to package materials and how to market themselves much better than others. Some may have had more experience at preparing portfolios, especially those from teacher training programs that use portfolios for their students. Some may have access to superior resources, such as experienced videotaping personnel or color laser printers, that allow them to assemble much more polished products. Some teachers may have coaches available to help them with the process, while others have to work in isolation or in a group with others who are inexperienced with portfolios. Bird (1990) points out that, "When the stakes in evaluation are high, they [the teachers] may be led to polish the documentation to a degree that is out of proportion to its function and importance, or even to misrepresent its source" (p. 244).

In high-stake situations, cheating and plagiarism may and probably will occur. Portfolio items may reflect, not what the teacher does, but what the teacher says he/she does. Administrative procedures must specify what assistance is allowed, what resources can be used, what action will be taken if cheating or plagiarism occur, and what training scorers and evaluators will be given so that they are not unduly influenced by appearance and packaging, and are alert to possible cases of cheating and plagiarism.

The cost of using portfolios can be high and can easily get out of hand. These costs can include time, money, and resources for the teacher, for the school, and for the students. Given the limited resources available to most teachers, teacher motivation plays a major role in the amount of effort devoted to compiling and using a portfolio. Schools must consider costs associated with training scorers to be accurate and consistent over time, the process of scoring the items, space and equipment for storing materials in a secure manner, and updating the items in the portfolios as needed.

Opportunity costs should be considered. If the resources devoted to portfolios get out of hand, students can suffer. A teacher may spend more time developing elaborate lesson plans (if they are desirable items for the portfolio) and little time giving feedback to students or monitoring their progress. Teachers can easily become overly-ambitious in preparing their portfolios, thus overtaxing their energy and interfering with their teaching responsibilities.

Portfolios can become unduly time-consuming and even a useless paper chase if not implemented properly. Based on his review of the literature, Wolf (1990) concluded that, "Previous efforts as assessing teachers through portfolios in licensure and career ladder programs in Tennessee and Florida, for example, indicated that if the portfolio task is too open-ended or ill-defined then the task easily can turn to a paper chase. The portfolios that the teachers submitted in these previous ventures were unmanageably large and unfocused" (p. 18).

Potential disadvantages include lack of representativeness of portfolio items, impact of portfolios appearance on scoring, cheating and plagiarism, high costs to compile and to score, and the possibility of becoming a useless paper chase and a futile exercise.

CONCLUSIONS

Portfolios, when used for assessing teacher performance, are a new approach compared to the more traditional ones, especially classroom observations. They can be a valuable addition as a source of evidence on teaching performance. In discussing approaches to teacher performance assessment, Shulman (1988) points out,

> Each of these several approaches to the assessment of teachers is, in itself, as fundamentally flawed as it is reasonably suitable, as perilously insufficient as it is peculiarly fitting. What we need, therefore, is a union of insufficiencies, a marriage of complements, in which the flaws of individual approaches to assessment are offset by the virtues of their fellows. (p. 38)

Although portfolios can be separate from other processes used for teacher development, assessment, and evaluation, they can be useful adjuncts to such processes. They provide a means of collecting samples of various materials that reflect professional development of the teacher over time. They can be used both by the teacher for reflection and individual development, as well as by a mentor or support-provider or trainer to monitor change over time and to plan professional development activities for a teacher. The materials in the portfolio can be used for self-evaluation and also as assessment instruments to be scored for possible use in teacher evaluation.

A portfolio also provides materials for other assessment activities (e.g., background information for an observer, stimulus materials for an interview). The portfolio can be useful in the evaluation process, not only as source of assessment data and information used in this process, but also to provide supporting documentation and evidence for judgments made and for verifying other assessment data and information. When used with interviews or conferences, portfolios make possible an informed conversation about one's own teaching. This encourages teachers to reflect on and critique their own behavior, a process that usually leads to improved performance. It also provides the evaluator with a more solid basis upon which to make informed judgments and decisions.

Simply collecting materials for a portfolio is of little value; the value lies in the use of the portfolio with other assessment, development, and evaluation processes. Portfolios should be used in conjunction with other assessment approaches "as well as a source of evidence not available through other approaches. Portfolio are flawed . . . , but no other method of assessment can equal them in providing a connection to the contexts and personal histories of real teaching" (Wolf, 1991a, p. 136).

Many schools and teacher training programs are using portfolios in a low-stakes manner at this time, primarily for professional development, self-evaluation, and teacher training. Tierney (1992) states that, ". . . moving toward the use of teacher portfolios as a means of assessing teachers for certification or employment seems premature and fraught with danger" (p. 21).

Schools and districts that want to use portfolios as part of the teacher evaluation process should proceed with caution. As a start, they should try using them for professional development and for encouraging teacher self-evaluation and reflection. By having much more information on what is feasible to include, portfolios can be designed to be more useful for understanding teacher performance in various job assignments and school contexts. They then can be scored more accurately and interpreted in more meaningful ways. Portfolios can make a worthwhile contribution not only to the evaluation process, but also to the improvement of teaching and instruction for all students. Once they are accepted and teachers have some experience compiling them, portfolio use in professional development, assessment, and performance evaluation can be more fully implemented.

Author's Note: The author acknowledges the following educators for their helpful comments on and additions to earlier versions of this paper: Vanna Born, Livermore (CA) Valley Joint Unified School District; Geneva D. Haertel, CREATE, Western Michigan University; Joanne Savage, East Side (San Jose, CA) Union High School District; Dennis S. Tierney, San Jose State University; Bill Trost, Shaker Heights City (OH) School District; and Kenneth Wolf, University of Colorado at Denver.

The preparation of this document was partially supported under the Educational Research and Development Center Program Grant Award Number R117000047 as administered by the Office of Educational Research and Improvement (OERI) of the U.S. Department of Education (USED). The inclusion of an item in this document does not necessarily represent approval of its contents or endorsement of its use by CREATE, OERI, or USED.

BIBLIOGRAPHY

This list provides not only the references in this paper, but others that may be of interest.

Arter, Judith. A; & Spandel, Vicki. (1992, Spring). Using portfolios of student work in instruction. *Educational Measurement: Issues and Practice, 11*(1), 36–44.

Berry, David; Kisch, June; Ryan, Charles; & Uphoff, James. (1991, April). *The process and product of portfolio construction.* Paper presented at the annual meeting of the American Educational Research Association, Chicago, IL.

Biddle, Jim; & Lasley, Thomas. (1991, April). *Portfolios and the process of teacher education.* Paper presented at the annual meeting of the American Educational Research Association, Chicago, IL.

Bird, Tom. (1990). The schoolteacher's portfolio: An essay on possibilities. In Jason Millman & Linda Darling-Hammond (Eds.), *The new handbook of teacher evaluation: Assessing elementary and secondary school teachers* (pp. 241–256). Newbury Park, CA: Sage Publications, Inc.

Black, Susan. (1993, February). Portfolio assessment. *The Executive Educator, 15*(1), 28–31.

Brauchle, Paul E.; McLarty, Joyce R.; & Parker, James. (1989, December). A portfolio approach to using student performance data to measure teacher effectiveness. *Journal of Personnel Evaluation in Education, 3*(1), 17–30. (ERIC Document Reproduction Service No. EJ 412 517)

Calfee, Robert C.; & Perfumo, Pam. (1993, April). *Student portfolios and teacher logs: Blueprint for a revolution in assesment* (Technical Report No. 65). Berkeley, CA: University of California at Berkeley, National Center for the Study of Writing.

Cole, Donna; Messner, P.; Swonigan, Howard; & Tillman, Beverly. (1991, April 6). *Portfolio structure and student profiles: An analysis of education student portfolio reflectivity scores.* Paper presented at the annual meeting of the American Educational Research Association, Chicago, IL.

Collins, Angelo. (1990a). *A teacher's portfolio—What is necessary and sufficient? (A high school biology unit as an example).* New York, NY: Carnegie Corporation. (ERIC Document Reproduction Service No. ED 319 814)

Collins, Angelo. (1990b). *Novices, experts, veterans, and masters: The role of content and pedagogical knowledge in evaluating teachers.* New York, NY: Carnegie Corporation. (ERIC Document Reproduction Service No. ED 319 815)

Collins, Angelo. (1990c, April). *Transforming the assesment of teachers: Notes on a theory of assessment for the 21st century.* Paper based on a presentation at the annual meeting of the National Catholic Education Association, Toronto, Canada. (ERIC Document Reproduction Service No. ED 321 362)

Collins, Angelo. (1991, October). Portfolios for biology teacher assessment. *Journal of Personnel Evaluation in Education, 5*(2), 147–168.

Edgerton, Russell. (1991, March 26). *The teaching portfolio as a display of best work.* Paper presented at the National Conference on Higher Education of the American Association for Higher Education, Washington, DC.

Edgerton, Russell; Hutchings, Patricia; & Quinlan, Kathleen. (1991). *The teaching portfolio: Capturing the scholarship in teaching*. Washington, DC: American Association for Higher Education.

Far West Laboratory for Educational Research and Development. (1993, January). Teaching portfolios: Synthesis of research and annotated bibliography. *Executive Summary, 1*(1), 32–34.

Haertel, Edward H. (1986, Spring). The valid use of student performance measures for teacher evaluation. *Educational Evaluation and Policy Analysis, 8*(1), 45–60. (ERIC Document Reproduction Service No. EJ 350 184)

Herman, Joan L.; Aschbacher, Pamela R.; & Winters, Lynn. (1992). *A practical guide to alternative assessment*. Alexandria, VA: Association for Supervision and Curriculum Development.

Koretz, Daniel M.; Stecher, Brian M.; Klein, Stephen P.; McCaffrey, Daniel; Bell, Robert; Harrison, Ellen; Diebert, Edward; & Hamilton, Eric. (forthcoming). *The Vermont Portfolio Assessment Program: An evaluation of the first state-wide implementation, 1991–92*. Santa Monica, CA: The RAND Corporation.

McRobbie, Joan. (1992). *Using portfolios to assess student performance* (Knowledge Brief No. 9). San Francisco, CA: Far West Laboratory for Educational Research and Development.

National Board for Professional Teaching Standards. (1991). *Toward high and rigorous standards for the teaching profession* (3rd ed.). Washington, DC: Author.

Scriven, Michael. (1988, March 13). *Evaluating teachers as professionals*. Unpublished manuscript. (ERIC Document Reproduction Service No. ED 300 882)

Scriven, Michael. (1991, September). *Duties of the teacher* (TEMP Memo 5). Kalamazoo, MI: Western Michigan University, The Evaluation Center, Center for Research on Educational Accountability and Teacher Evaluation.

Seldin, Peter. (1991). *The teaching portfolio: A practical guide to improved performance and promotion/tenure decisions*. Boston, MA: Anker Publishing.

Shulman, Lee S. (1987, September). Assessment for teaching: An initiative for the profession. *Phi Delta Kappan, 69*(1), 38–44. (ERIC Document Reproduction Service No. EJ 359 287)

Shulman, Lee S. (1988, November). A union of insufficiencies: Strategies for teacher assessment in a period of educational reform. *Educational Leadership, 46*(3), 36–41. (ERIC Document Reproduction Service No. EJ 385 344)

Shulman, Lee S. (1991, June). *Keynote address*. Paper presented at the Third National Forum of the National Board for Professional Teaching Standards, St. Louis, MO.

Terry, Gwenith L.; & Eade, Gordon E. (1983). *The portfolio process: New roles for meeting challenges in professional development.* Paper presented at the annual conference of the Association of Teacher Educators, Pensacola, FL. (ERIC Document Reproduction Service No. ED 229 342)

Tierney, Dennis S. (1992). *Teaching portfolios: 1992 update on research and practice.* San Francisco, CA: Far West Laboratory for Educational Research and Development.

Vavrus, Linda; & Calfee, Robert. (1988). *A research strategy for assessing teachers of elementary literacy: The promise of performance portfolios.* Paper presented at the annual meeting of the National Reading Conference, Tucson, AZ.

Vavrus, Linda; & Collins, Angelo. (1991, Summer). Portfolio documentation and assessment center exercises: A marriage made for teacher assessment. *Teacher Education Quarterly, 18*(3), 13–39.

Wheeler, Patricia. (1993). *Methods for assessing performance* (EREAPA Publication Series No. 93-6). Livermore, CA: EREAPA Associates.

Wheeler, Patricia; & Haertel, Geneva D. (1993). *A resource handbook on performance assessment and measurement: A tool for students, practitioners, and policymakers.* Berkeley, CA: The Owl Press.

Wheeler, Patricia; Haertel, Geneva D.; & Scriven, Michael. (1992). *Teacher evaluation glossary.* Kalamazoo, MI: Western Michigan University, The Evaluation Center, Center for Research on Educational Accountability and Teacher Evaluation.

Wolf, Kenneth. (1990a, June). *Evaluating teacher knowledge and skills in student assessment through teacher portfolios* (TAP Technical Report No. L2). Stanford, CA: Stanford University, School of Education, Teacher Assessment Project.

Wolf, Kenneth. (1990b). *The schoolteacher's portfolio: Practical issues in design, implementation, and evaluation* (TAP Technical Report No. N1). Stanford, CA: Stanford University, School of Education, Teacher Assessment Project.

Wolf, Kenneth P. (1991a, October). The schoolteacher's portfolio: Issues in design, implementation, and evaluation. *Phi Delta Kappan, 73*(2), 129–136.

Wolf, Kenneth P. (1991b, November). *Teaching portfolios: Synthesis of research and annotated bibliography.* San Francisco, CA: Far West Laboratory for Educational Research and Development.

Wolf, Kenneth Paul; et al. (1988, December 2). *Designing portfolios for the assessment of elementary literacy teaching: Work-in-progress.* Paper presented at the annual meeting of the National Reading Conference, Tucson, AZ. (ERIC Document Reproduction Service No. ED 302 842)

The Use of Portfolios in Assessing Teacher Competence: Measurement Issues

by Estelle S. Gellman

I t is abundantly clear that teaching is too complex an activity to be assessed with tests alone. Tests may be adequate for the evaluation of some of the knowledge that is a necessary component of effective teaching but we need additional assessment techniques to determine whether that knowledge is reflected in appropriate teaching behavior.

Although tests have been the traditional mode of assessment in many teacher-education courses and tests such as the National Teacher Examinations are often used as criteria for entry into the profession, tests are rarely used as the mode of assessing the teaching proficiency of either pre-service or practicing teachers. Instead, most school districts employ some type of observation procedure. As opposed to tests, observation enables the evaluator to directly assess the performance of the teacher in the classroom. There are several problems, however, that are associated with observation. Although there are some highly developed observation instruments, such as the North Carolina Teaching Appraisal Instrument, most teacher observation instruments are highly informal (Gellman & Berkowitz, 1989). Although, on the surface, one might expect observation instruments to provide more valid assessments of teacher performance that paper and pencil tests, these forms of assessment also raise serious questions of both validity and reliability.

From *Action in Teacher Education*, vol. 14, no. 4, Winter 1992–1993, pp. 39–44. © 1992 by the Association of Teacher Educators. Reprinted with permission.

Aside from the basic validity issue of whether teacher evaluation instruments are assessing the critical aspects of teacher performance, Soar, Medley and Coker (1983) argue that assessment procedures should have four basic attributes: they should present each individual being assessed with a standard task, they should provide a record of performance, they should have an agreed upon scoring key, and they should have publicly available standards against which an individual's performance can be measured. Most of the traditional modes of teacher evaluation, however, do not meet these criteria. Teachers are observed teaching widely different types of lessons to markedly different students. The teaching behaviors to be rated are vaguely defined and are subject to wide interpretation. Although some observation instruments are designed to leave a record of performance, the record of the observation is usually a general subjective reaction based upon the values of the observer. Furthermore, the observation is usually performed by a single supervisor on a single occasion. It provides a "snapshot" of performance and often a snapshot of the teacher's best performance. It cannot indicate whether this level of performance persists over time nor whether it is representative of the teacher's performance at other times, in other classes or on other lessons. Although there may be an agreed upon scoring key—in the sense of whether a teacher will be rated on a three-point scale of poor, average, or outstanding, for example, or whether a list of behaviors will be checked as present or absent—there tends to be little more than cursory attention given to assuring that these ratings have the same meaning for different raters. Furthermore, published norms are almost nonexistent.

> Dissatisfaction with traditional methods of evaluating teacher performance has spurred investigation of alternate modes of assessment.

Dissatisfaction with these traditional methods of evaluating teaching performance has spurred investigation of alternate modes of assessment, with portfolio assessment receiving much current interest. In their investigation of new approaches to teacher evaluation, the Teacher Assessment Project (TAP) at Stanford University, for example, has explored the use of both portfolios and simulation exercises at assessment centers (Collins, 1990a, 1990b, 1990c; Shulman, 1988; Wolf, 1988, 1991). The Florida State Board of Education specifies that a portfolio be maintained for beginning teachers in their Beginning Teacher Program (Terry, Backman & Eade, 1983; Terry & Eade, 1983; University of South Florida, 1986a, 1986b) and many pre-service teacher education programs, such as that of Bowling Green State University (Weinberger & Didham, 1987), the University of Dayton (Geiger & Sugarman, 1988), Hofstra University (Miletta, 1992), and Long Island University (Pascale, 1992) are using portfolio assessment in their teacher-education programs.

In describing the portfolio assessment process, several advantages have been cited for this mode of evaluation. In examining theses advantages, however, it is important to differentiate between those benefits that reflect the qualities of good pedagogy and those that reflect the qualities of good assessment (although, of course, they do not necessarily have to be mutually exclusive). In citing the advantages of the portfolios, Shulman (1988), for example, argues that portfolios can document the unfolding of teaching and learning over time as well as provide teachers the opportunity to engage in the analysis of what they have done. While the ability to document growth in performance over time is most certainly related to the validity of a teacher assessment instrument, the ability for the teacher to engage in analysis, while it may be beneficial, does not necessarily pertain to the validity or reliability of the process as a mode of evaluation. This advantage of the portfolio is only relevant to the measurement qualities of portfolio assessment if we specifically wish to assess the teacher's ability to engage in such analysis. Similarly, although several studies have indicated that portfolios may be helpful for prospective teachers in seeking initial employment (Miletta, 1992; Weinberger & Didham, 1987; Williamson & Abel, 1989), this advantage, also, does not relate to the quality of the assessments made through the examination of portfolios. The basic question, then, is what it is that we want to assess and whether portfolio assessment is a more valid and reliable process for measuring these qualities than are other available methods. A second, related question is whether we are concerned with summative or formative evaluation.

Let us first consider the issue of validity, the question of whether a measurement instrument is, in fact, assessing that which we want to assess. Different teacher education programs and different school districts will obviously differ in the importance that they attach to different factors in a teacher's performance. The point of this paper is not to specify what should be assessed, however, but to emphasize the importance of determining what it is that you want to assess in a particular situation. As with any measurement procedure, one particular portfolio assessment procedure will not be valid in every situation. A process appropriate for elementary school reading teachers may not be appropriate for secondary school teachers of science. A teacher education program that emphasizes reflective practice, for example, may require very different types of portfolio entries than a program with a different approach.

> As with any measurement procedure, one particular portfolio assessment procedure will not be valid in every situation.

Given that the outcomes to be assessed have been defined, the issue then becomes the type of outcome for which portfolio assessment is valid. In the same way that an essay examination would provide a more valid assessment of a student's ability to organize material and communicate clearly in his or [her] own words than would a multiple choice test, portfolio assessment would seem to have advantages in assessing those characteristics of teaching that cannot be measured by a paper or pencil test or observed in a limited observation period.

From the standpoint of validity, portfolio assessment has the advantage of enabling the evaluation of a much larger and more varied sample of teacher performance than would an observation. Consider, for example, the array of documents that have been included in portfolios. In the TAP (Collins, 1990a, 1990c; Wolf, 1991), for example, portfolios included (1) actual artifacts of teaching and learning, such as lesson plans, student work and test materials, (2) the teacher's reflections and analyses of these activities and products, and (3) videotapes of lessons. The portfolios piloted by the University of West Florida (Terry & Eade, 1983) include, in addition to documents such as those in the TAP, results of observations as well as evidence of a plan for improvement. Although much of the information included in these portfolios could be obtained through observation coupled with teacher conferences, the advantage of the portfolio is that it can more concisely document a wider variety of activities taking place in a greater number of settings over a longer period of time. It appears to be capable of providing a more representative sample of performance than can be evaluated in a limited observation period and to provide a more authentic measure of teacher performance.

> In the Teacher Assessment Project at Stanford, the portfolios are augmented by simulated exercises in an assessment center.

Cizek (1991) warns, however, that we cannot rely solely on face validity; we need more evidence of validity than that a process "appears" or "looks" as if it [is] assessing those tasks that we wish to assess. There is nothing in the literature on portfolio assessment, however, that indicates that we cannot also obtain data on the concurrent or predictive validity of the assessment in a particular setting. Indeed, in the Teacher Assessment Project at Stanford, the portfolios are augmented by simulated exercises in an assessment center (Shulman, 1988; Wolf, 1991). Why couldn't evidence of concurrent validity be obtained by examining the relationship between the portfolio assessments and the assessments made of the same teachers' performance in the simulation exercises? Or, why couldn't the portfolio assessments be examined in relationship to the evaluations the teachers received in their respective schools? At the University of Dayton, Geiger & Sugarman (1988) report that both portfolios and case studies have been used to supplement traditional methods of assessing students in their teacher education programs. In this instance, also, an estimate of concurrent validity could be obtained by examining the students' standing on both types of assessment. Similarly, in those situations where portfolio assessment is a factor in hiring, an assessment of predictive validity could be obtained by correlating the portfolio assessments with subsequent teacher evaluations. We cannot determine on an *a priori* basis that portfolio assessment is valid in a particular situation. It is incumbent upon us to provide the same type of evidence of concurrent and predictive validity for portfolio assessment as for any other type of assessment technique. There is nothing in the process, however, that indicates that such evidence for validity would not be forthcoming.

Before we can establish evidence of validity, however, we must demonstrate that our measurements are reliable. The Soar, Medley and Coker (1983) critique of assessment methods cited earlier identifies many of the reliability issues that must be examined in regard to assessing teacher performance. Although portfolio assessment does not satisfy all of their criteria, there are steps that can be taken to improve the reliability of such assessment.

Although portfolios are very personal and idiosyncratic in many respects, they can be prepared to respond to a standard task or set of tasks.

Although portfolios are very personal and idiosyncratic in many respects, they can be prepared to respond to a standard task or set of tasks. In the Teacher Assessment Project at Stanford (Wolf et al., 1988), for example, three areas were identified for documentation in the elementary literacy project: (1) teaching and planning integrated language instruction, (2) the assessment of students, and (3) creating a literate environment. Wolf (1988) further indicates that, in order to document planning and teaching, teachers were asked to provide (a) an overview of three to five weeks of instruction, (b) details of two to three consecutive lessons, (c) a roster of literary works and other resources selected for use, (d) copies of handouts, (e) samples of student work, and (f) videotapes of three different forms of instruction: a large group literature activity; a small group discussion; and one-to-one writing conferences with two students of different skills levels.

In preparing such portfolios there will obviously be wide disparities in the specific material submitted or there will be different lessons, different student works, different resources, and so on. Nevertheless, if there is a common set of criteria on which to judge this set of products, and if there is adequate inter-rater reliability in the judgments of the raters, one may obtain an acceptable level of reliability.

When portfolio assessment is addressed in the manner described in the Teacher Assessment Project (Wolf, 1991), for example, it would appear to be a mode of assessment that meets most of the criteria set forth by Soar, Medley and Coker (1983): although the products differ, each individual being assessed is provided with a standard task; portfolios do provide a record of performance; and they do have an agreed upon scoring key or even though the scores are subjective, there nevertheless appears to be considerable agreement and clarity on the performance criteria.

> **No matter how reliable a multiple-choice test may be, it has inherent limitations in terms of its validity for assessing teaching proficiency.**

There is no reason why such practices cannot be duplicated in other settings; the fact that many proponents of portfolio assessment have not yet focused on issues of reliability does not mean that this method of assessment is inherently suspect in comparison to multiple choice tests or observations of teaching behavior. Consider for just a minute how many professors of teacher education you know that assess the reliability and validity of the paper and pencil tests—both subjective and objective—that they regularly give to students in the form of midterm or final examinations. Furthermore, no matter how reliable a multiple-choice test may be, it has inherent limitations in terms of its validity for assessing teaching proficiency.

Portfolio assessment, of course, also has its limitations. Concerns have [been] raised, for example, about how we can be sure that the portfolio entries represent the individual's own work and the extent to which assessment may focus on how the portfolio is packaged as opposed to the depth of the work presented. As indicated by Shulman (1988) and Wolf (1991), the issue of whether the portfolio represents the teacher's own work can be addressed through follow-up interviews and/or discussions of the work in which teachers are, for example, asked how they would modify particular lessons in response to various interventions, or by comparing the nature of the entries with performance during classroom observations, tests or simulated activities. The question of "gloss versus depth" is analogous to the old question of the extent to which handwriting enters into the scores on essay examinations. There is no way of taking the subjectivity out of portfolio analysis and there is no doubt that a sloppy presentation will probably detract from the assessment. One would expect, however, that attention to this issue when focusing on the performance criteria would diminish the effect. Portfolio assessment is not a panacea that will solve all the problems of performance measurement and it will be subject to all the caveats that are raised in regard to subjective ratings. The case for portfolio assessment does not rest on the fact that it will necessarily provide a more reliable mode of assessing teaching proficiency but that it has the capability of adding to the validity of our assessments if adequate attention is given to these measurement issues.

> Portfolio assessment is not a panacea that will solve all the problems of performance measurement.

Additionally, if we want an assessment method that not only evaluates final achievement but also enables us to document progress and provide appropriate intervention, it would seem that portfolio assessment is ideally suited to meet this need. Indeed, in many instances where portfolio assessment is in use (Elbow & Belanoff, 1986; McKee, 1992; Miletta, 1992; Shulman, 1988), it is this formative function that has been advocated. It is a method of assessment that does not necessarily require all students to reach the same level of proficiency in a particular skill at the same time. If we have a process whereby we periodically examine each student's portfolio entries, we have the opportunity to provide feedback and guidance to the student on a regular basis. Although, of course, this sharing of information could also be based upon regular observations or tests, the advantage of the portfolio is that it allows for the assessment of performance in a wide array of tasks that would be difficult to assess through either observation or a test and it is more conserving of time than observation. Furthermore, it is a technique that enables us to work on each student's different strengths and weaknesses on an individual basis, without regard to where other students may be on a particular skill in reference to other students. At Stony Brook University, for example, Elbow and Belanoff (1986) report that in replacing writing proficiency examinations with portfolios they have moved to a criterion-referenced model of evaluation, the outcome of which is to put the teacher in the role of coach with the goal of helping all students to eventually meet the criterion.

The pedagogical benefits of using portfolios may accrue regardless of whether or not the assessment process is sound from a measurement perspective. These benefits may, in and of themselves, argue for the use of portfolios in teacher education and other professional preparation programs. If we wish to use portfolio assessment for the evaluation of professional proficiency, however, we must take steps to assure that the procedure that we use meets appropriate criteria of both reliability and validity. In order to do so, considerable attention must be given to the determination of what aspects of performance should be measured, what type of evidence would exemplify proficiency, how the evidence will be rated, who the raters will be and how they will be trained. Portfolio assessment may not be the answer to all of our assessment dreams but, where appropriate attention is given to issues of reliability and validity, it can become a valuable tool in assessing professional competence.

REFERENCES

Cizek, G. J. (1991, May). Innovation or ennervation. *Phi Delta Kappan*, 695–699.

Collins, A. (1990a). *A teacher's portfolio—What is necessary and sufficient?* (A high school biology unit plan as an example). NY: Carnegie Corp. of NY. (ERIC Document Reproduction Service No. ED 319 814)

Collins, A. (1990b). *Novices, experts, veterans, and masters: The role of content and pedagogical knowledge in evaluating teaching.* NY: Carnegie Corp. of NY. (ERIC Document Reproduction Service No. 319 815)

Collins, A. (1990c). *Transforming the assessment of teachers: Notes on a theory of assessment for the 21st century.* NY: Carnegie Corp. of NY. (ERIC Document Reproduction Service No. 321 362)

Elbow, P., & Belanoff, P. (1986). Portfolios as a substitute for proficiency examination. *College Composition and Communication, 37*, 336–339.

Geiger, J., & Sugarman, S. (1988). Portfolios and case studies to evaluate teacher education students and programs. *Action in Teacher Education, 31*(3), 31–34.

Gellman, E., & Berkowitz, M. (1989, October). *A descriptive analysis of currently used teacher evaluation instruments.* Paper presented at the annual meeting of the Northeastern Educational Research Association, Ellenville, NY.

McKee, J. C. (1992, March). *Use of the portfolio in teacher education.* Paper presented at the annual meeting of the Eastern Educational Research Association, Hilton Head, SC.

Miletta, M. (1992, March). Implementing portfolio/process assessment with student teachers: A suburban university. In M. Berkowitz (Chair), *Portfolio/process assessment: Theory and practice.* Symposium conducted at the meeting of the Eastern Educational Research Association, Hilton Head, SC.

Pascale, I. (1992, March). Implementing portfolio/process assessment with student teachers: An urban university. In M. Berkowitz (Chair), *Portfolio/process assessment: Theory and practice.* Symposium conducted at the meeting of the Eastern Educational Research Association, Hilton Head, SC.

Shulman, L. S. (1988). A union of insufficiencies: Strategies for teacher assessment in a period of educational reform. *Educational Leadership, 46*(3), 36–41.

Soar, R. S., Medley, D. M., & Coker, H. (1983, December). Teacher evaluation: A critique of currently used methods. *Phi Delta Kappan,* 239–246.

Terry, G. L., Backman, C. A., & Eade, G. E. (1983). *The portfolio process in professional development.* Pensacola, FL: The University of West Florida. (ERIC Document Reproduction Service No. ED 227 073)

Terry, G., & Eade, G. E. (1983). *The portfolio process: New roles for meeting challenges in professional development.* Pensacola, FL: The University of West Florida. (ERIC Document Reproduction Service No. ED 229 342)

University of South Florida. (1986a). *A study of beginning teacher portfolios.* Tampa: University of South Florida, Tampa College of Education and Tallahassee: Florida State Dept. of Education. (ERIC Document Reproduction Service No. ED 277 689)

University of South Florida. (1986b). *An exploratory study of the relationships between beginning teachers' professional development programs and their performance as measured by the FPMS.* Tampa: University of South Florida, Tampa College of Education and Tallahassee: Florida State Dept. of Education. (ERIC Document Reproduction Service No. ED 277 689)

Weinberger, H., & Didham, C. K. (1987). *Helping prospective teachers sell themselves: The portfolio as a marketing strategy.* Bowling Green, OH: Bowling Green State University. (ERIC Document Reproduction Service No. 278 639)

Williamson, R. E., & Abel, F. J. (1989). *The professional portfolio: Keys to a successful job search for the beginning teacher.* Mount Berry, GA: Berry College. (ERIC Document Reproduction Service No. ED 304 418)

Wolf, K. P., Athanases, S., & Chin, E. (1988, December). *Designing portfolios for the assessment of elementary literacy teaching: Work-in-progress.* (ERIC Document Reproduction Service No. ED 302 842)

Wolf, K. (1991, October). The schoolteacher's portfolio: Issues in design, implementation, and evaluation. *Phi Delta Kappan,* 129–136.

The Schoolteacher's Portfolio: Issues in Design, Implementation, and Evaluation

by Kenneth Wolf

The Teacher Assessment Project (TAP) at Stanford University recently completed a four-year effort to explore and develop new approaches to teacher evaluation. The resulting methods and prototypes were intended to assist the National Board for Professional Teaching Standards in its creation of a voluntary program for the national certification of teachers for elementary and secondary schools.[1] TAP focused on two approaches in particular: simulation exercises, performed at assessment centers, and portfolios, which offer teachers the opportunity to document their actual teaching.[2]

As strategies for assessing teachers' pedagogical competence, both approaches possess virtues as well as limitations. Portfolios, the focus of this article, hold great promise for teacher evaluation but are fraught with potential problems. Portfolios are messy to construct, cumbersome to store, difficult to score, and vulnerable to misrepresentation. But, in ways that no other assessment method can, portfolios provide a connection to the contexts and personal histories of real teaching and make it possible to document the unfolding of both teaching and learning over time.[3]

BACKGROUND

The TAP research was carried out in two main phases over a four-year period. In the first phase of this investigation of alter-

From *Phi Delta Kappan,* vol. 73, no. 2, October 1991, pp. 129–36. © 1991 by Phi Delta Kappa. Reprinted with permission.

native methods of teacher assessment, members of the TAP staff designed assessment center exercises in two subject-matter

Assessment center exercises and the contents of portfolios were developed with the perspectives and practices of specific subject-matter areas in mind.

areas: elementary mathematics and high school history. Forty teachers, twenty each in math and history, volunteered to participate in three days of assessment center activities, in which they were asked, for example, to plan and teach a lesson to a small group of students, to critique a textbook, to respond to examples of student work, and to review a videotape of another teacher's lesson as a stimulus for reflecting on their own teaching.[4]

The second phase of the TAP research focused on compiling portfolios and dealt with a different pair of subject-matter areas— elementary literacy and high school biology. Twenty teachers in elementary literacy and twenty in biology documented their teaching for one school year through such materials as videotapes, lesson plans, samples of student work, and reflective commentaries. In an attempt to link the portfolio and assessment center work, the literacy and biology teams also developed assessment center exercises that were based on the activities documented in a teacher's portfolio.[5]

A central assumption of the project was that "the *subject matters*" (to borrow the title of a book by Susan Stodolsky).[6] Assessment center exercises and the contents of portfolios were developed with the perspectives and practices of specific subject-matter areas in mind. In the teaching of history, for example, primary documents play a vital role; in science, a laboratory lesson presents an entirely different set of instructional problems and possibilities.

In addition, the TAP development teams, composed of both practicing teachers and university researchers, received substantial teacher input during all phases of their investigations. A review panel of teachers evaluated the design of the portfolios and assessment center exercises, consulting teachers tried out early versions of the materials, and teachers who took part in the field test provided ongoing feedback about their experiences in constructing portfolios and completing assessment center exercises.

PRACTICAL ISSUES IN DEVELOPING PORTFOLIOS

In conducting their investigation of portfolios, the elementary literacy and high school biology teams followed similar sequences of events. Each team identified a number of critical teaching tasks in its respective subject area, designed portfolio entries around these tasks, assisted classroom teachers as they constructed their portfolios, supervised an assessment center in which teachers discussed their portfolios and completed exercises, and evaluated the teachers' performances. This entire process was informed by the participation of a diverse and knowledgeable group of teachers and scholars. Practicing teachers guided the development of the portfolios from inception to completion; researchers and teacher educators in literacy and biology assisted in designing and evaluating the portfolios; minority teachers and scholars raised concerns and offered suggestions for addressing issues of equity and diversity.

> Practicing teachers guided the development of the portfolios from inception to completion.

In the course of designing, implementing, and evaluating assessment center exercises and portfolio entries, participants in the project wrestled with both policy-related and practical issues. While these concerns overlap and are inseparable to some degree, I will focus primarily on the practicalities of developing a teacher's portfolio. What is important for teachers to document? What form should a portfolio take? What kinds of evidence should go into a portfolio? How much evidence should be included?

1. *What is a schoolteacher's portfolio?* On one level, a schoolteacher's portfolio can be defined as a container for storing and displaying evidence of a teacher's knowledge and skills. However, this definition is incomplete. A portfolio is more than a container—a portfolio also embodies an attitude that assessment is dynamic and that the richest portrayals of teacher (and student) performance are based on multiple sources of evidence collected over time in authentic settings.[7]

We began with the premise that any system of teacher assessment must faithfully reflect the richness and complexities of teaching and learning. While various methods of assessment—

such as written tests, direct observations, and assessment center exercises—can provide multiple views of a teacher's competence, we believed that many important dimensions of teaching and learning could be captured only through portfolios. As Lee Shulman observes, portfolios "retain almost uniquely the potential for documenting the unfolding of both teaching and learning over time and combining that documentation with opportunities for teachers to engage in the analysis of what they and their students have done."[8]

2. *What purposes can a portfolio serve?* In the past, teachers documented their teaching for one of two reasons: either they had been nominated for an award and needed to show evidence of excellence, or they had been threatened with dismissal and had to provide proof of their competence. But few teachers fall into these two categories. The vast majority of teachers have no compelling reason to document their teaching. For what other purposes, then, might teachers want to prepare a portfolio?

> The vast majority of teachers have no compelling reason to document their teaching.

The TAP research explored the role that portfolios can play in the voluntary national certification of accomplished teachers. A portfolio that includes, for example, samples of student work, teacher-developed plans and materials, videotaped teaching episodes, and the teacher's reflections on his or her own teaching can provide direct evidence of what a teacher knows and can do. In combination with evidence from other sources, such as written tests and direct observations, this portfolio could be the basis for recognizing and rewarding excellence in the field of teaching. While the primary focus of the TAP research was on the role that portfolios can play in the evaluation of schoolteachers, it is important to keep in mind that a teacher's portfolio can (and should) also serve such purposes as promoting the development of individual teachers and highlighting exemplary practices.

3. *What is important for teachers to document through their portfolios?* We began our research with two considerations in mind. First, we believed that a portfolio should reflect the important activities that take place in the classrooms of effective

teachers. That meant defining what is exemplary and essential
in the teaching of elementary literacy and high school biology.
Second, we wanted to determine the teaching activities that
were best suited for documentation and to explore various ways
of representing them through portfolios.

The development teams began by identifying critical tasks
in the teaching of elementary literacy and high school biology.
In arriving at this list of teaching tasks,
we were aware that, although teaching is
too complex to assess in its entirety, cutting it into little pieces destroys its integrity. In an effort to keep the teaching
"chunks" as whole and coherent as possible, we tried to avoid cutting at random
or sampling small bits of teaching. In addition, face validity was a concern. Not
only did these teaching tasks need to be
relatively large and meaningful; they also
had to be recognized by both teachers and the public as legitimate teaching activities.

> **The development teams began by identifying critical tasks in the teaching of elementary literacy and high school biology.**

Based on observations of exemplary teachers, reviews of
curriculum frameworks and research literature, and numerous
discussions with teachers and researchers, the literacy development team generated an extensive list of critical teaching tasks
in elementary literacy. From this initial list, they selected three
diverse teaching areas for documentation in portfolios: (1) integrated language instruction, (2) assessment of students, and (3)
creating a literate environment. While these categories addressed much of what is important in the teaching of elementary literacy, the three areas were not intended to cover the entire range of critical teaching tasks in literacy. Given that our
primary research responsibility was to explore the feasibility of
assessing teachers through portfolios, these aspects of instruction were chosen in part because they represented a diverse set
of challenges for documentation.

Each broad category was then subdivided into smaller,
more manageable tasks, each one of which became the basis for
a portfolio *entry*. The area of integrated language instruction
was broken down into "planning and adapting" and "teaching."
Assessment of students was divided into "initial," "ongoing,"

and "focused" assessment. Creating a literate environment included "classroom design" and "adapting and using the environment." A complete portfolio in elementary literacy was made up of separate, but complementary, entries for the seven tasks just mentioned, plus an "open" entry, in which the teacher could document an area of special interest or expertise, and a "background information" entry, in which teachers described the context in which they taught.

> In an effort to link the earlier TAP work with the present investigation of portfolios, the development teams also designed assessment center exercises.

The high school biology development team approached the problem of identifying critical teaching tasks in a different manner. They first identified four core tasks: (1) preparing and planning, (2) teaching, (3) evaluation and reflection, and (4) exchange with colleagues and with the community. Then they developed a list of documentable activities specific to biology within each of four broad areas of teaching: (1) unit planning, (2) conducting a lesson, (3) student evaluation, and (4) professional exchange. Conducting a lesson was further subdivided into entries for teaching a laboratory lesson or using alternative (nontextbook) materials, and professional exchange was broken down into entries for professional and community activities.

In an effort to link the earlier TAP work with the present investigation of portfolios, the development teams also designed assessment center exercises. We experimented with two different formats: "follow-up" exercises, using the teachers' own portfolios as the basis of the exercises, and free-standing exercises, which were independent of the experiences of any particular teacher.[9] Follow-up exercises enable teachers to draw on their own work and the context of their teaching in responding to typical teaching problems, while free-standing exercises provide a "level playing field" for all candidates. We developed these in part to see if exercises from one subject matter and grade level (e.g., elementary mathematics) could be adapted for use in others (e.g., high school biology) and in part to gain a better understanding of how the melding of portfolios and assessment center exercises contributes to an overall picture of a teacher's competence.

4. *What form should a portfolio take?* After selecting the specific areas to be documented within elementary literacy and high school biology, our next step was to explore various formats and procedures for representing these teaching tasks through portfolios. Early in the design process, we debated whether the teacher's portfolio should consist of the actual artifacts of teaching—such as lesson plans and samples of student work—or of the teacher's written reflections on the significance of the artifacts and events of classroom life.

> **Our next step was to explore various formats and procedures for representing these teaching tasks through portfolios.**

Some members of the development teams argued that conceptualizing the teacher's portfolio as a collection of classroom artifacts ran the risk of turning portfolio construction into an act of amassing paper. The portfolio could easily become a thick and unwieldy collection of documents and materials that would be indecipherable to anyone other than its owner. The portfolio as a collection of artifacts, they contended, would also present problems of storing and scoring. Keeping track and making sense of this huge collection of documents and materials would be an organizational nightmare. On the other hand, casting the portfolio as a collection of essays on teaching would distance it from what it is best at capturing—the raw material of teaching and learning. Focusing on a teacher's written statements would place a much greater emphasis on what teachers say they do in their classrooms than on what they actually do. Talk about teaching would be emphasized over the act of teaching.

We ultimately decided to have the teachers include both actual artifacts of teaching and learning and their written reflections on the meaning of these classroom activities and products. We felt that the artifacts alone would be relatively meaningless for evaluative purposes, while the reflective statements would be empty remarks if they weren't connected to the actual products of teaching and learning. Taken together, however, classroom artifacts, framed by the teacher's explanations and reflections, could provide an authentic and multitextured view of the actual

teaching that took place, as well as some insight into the thinking behind the teaching.

To prevent the portfolios from becoming unwieldy, we
tried to set clear purposes for documentation and specific limits
on the amount of evidence that could be
submitted for each portfolio entry. For
instance, the elementary literacy teachers
were instructed in one entry to "select
five to 10 pieces of evidence that illustrate your beginning-of-the-year literacy
assessment practices." To help ensure
that the documents and materials in the
portfolio would be meaningful to those
who reviewed them, we asked the teachers to attach brief, written captions identifying and explaining the purpose of each
piece of evidence. A caption might read, for example, "This
letter to my students' parents shows how I have tried to involve
parents in our literacy program." In addition to captioning the
evidence, the teachers also wrote reflective commentaries in
which they discussed what the contents of the portfolio revealed
about their teaching. In this approach, the portfolio is both
selective and reflective—carefully chosen artifacts of classroom
life are given meaning by the teacher's descriptions and
reflections.

> Schools do not
> normally provide
> teachers with the time
> or the opportunity
> for reflection.

In reviewing the completed portfolios, we learned that we
needed to provide more explicit guidelines for the reflective
statements. The teachers' commentaries were rich in description but generally lacked thoughtful analysis and interpretation.
We attributed the absence of reflection to both the nature of the
task and the culture of schools. While we now know that we
should have defined our expectations more clearly, we also recognize that schools do not normally provide teachers with the
time or the opportunity for reflection.[10] Stimulating deeper reflection will require more than a clear set of directions.

5. *What kinds of evidence should go into a portfolio?* Once
we decided that the portfolio should contain the "raw material"
of teaching, that these artifacts should be accompanied by captions, and that these captioned artifacts were even more meaningful when they were framed by the teacher's reflections and
rationales, our next task was to determine the particular kinds

of evidence that would best allow teachers to demonstrate what they know and do. We began by generating a list of documents and materials that teachers might provide in their portfolios. This list, intended to be suggestive rather than exhaustive, contained numerous examples of written documents, such as samples of student work, teacher logs or journals, published tests, lesson plans, text materials, and notes from parents. The list also included such nonprint materials as video- and audiotapes, photographs, and diagrams.

In our initial discussions about the possible contents of the portfolio, we debated whether to require the teachers to submit videotapes of their teaching. While we felt that videotapes were a potentially valuable source of evidence, we were concerned about the issue of access to video equipment and technical support. We ultimately decided to require all teachers to submit a videotape of their teaching, but, for the purposes of this research project, we sidestepped concerns about access by providing videotaping services to all teachers who requested them.

> A review of the portfolios suggested that the videotape . . . was one of the most important pieces of evidence.

A review of the portfolios suggested that the videotape, along with the teacher's descriptions and interpretations of the events on the tape, was one of the most important pieces of evidence.[11] The videotape allowed teaching to be seen in context as it changed in response to the students' needs and understanding. It revealed information beyond the scope of the particular lesson or event being taped—information about student participation, about the teacher's management strategies, about the school context. Most important[ly], the videotape provided an opportunity to evaluate both an actual teaching episode and, through the teacher's reflective statement and follow-up interview at the assessment center, the teacher's own assessment of that same event.

Videotaping does have drawbacks, however. It can be intrusive in a classroom, inspiring dramatic outbursts from the children and disrupting the normal flow of events. Moreover, unlike a teacher's written reflections about a particular teaching episode, which can provide a condensed representation of the event, a videotape conveys teaching in real time and, as a consequence, can be quite time-consuming to evaluate. In addition, the viewer may have the impression of having seen an uncensored teaching episode, when in reality the camera can conceal as well as reveal.

Overall, we found that the contents of the completed portfolios conformed closely to our suggested list. Some of the teachers submitted unusual pieces of evidence, such as a post-lesson analysis of an unsuccessful teaching episode, but most of the portfolios, not surprisingly, contained the familiar products of classroom life—student papers, lesson plans, and the like. One exception was the material used to document the task of creating a literate environment. For this section of the literacy portfolio, the teachers were directed to provide a diagram of the physical arrangement of the classroom, a videotaped tour of the classroom with narration, and captioned photographs of the children and the classroom. At a reunion one year after completing their portfolios, the teachers reported that this particular combination of documents was the most successful at engaging them in thinking about their literacy instruction as well as the most accurate in portraying their literacy programs.

> **Most of the portfolios contained the familiar products of classroom life—student papers, lesson plans, and the like.**

6. *How should the evidence in a portfolio be displayed?* One of our greatest fears was that we would get portfolios that had great visual appeal but little substance—portfolios that were neatly packaged and laminated but lacked clarity or coherence. In the handbooks on portfolio development and in our oral instructions to the teachers, therefore, we explained the need to be neat and legible but emphasized that we did not want the portfolios to be polished solely for the sake of display.

We encouraged a test case in biology. We received two portfolios that differed greatly in appearance—one was typed and written in complete sentences, the other written in pencil and replete with sentence fragments and cryptic notations. The typed portfolio contained numerous content errors, however, while the handwritten version conveyed a sound understanding of the subject matter. In the evaluations, the typed version was rated low and the handwritten one high. Apparently, the evaluators focused on the content of the portfolios. In this example, the disparity in subject-matter knowledge between the two teachers was quite apparent. But, if substantive differences were less pronounced, might appearance exert a subtle effect on evaluation?

While the issue of display needs closer investigation, a comparison of the portfolios that received exemplary ratings with those rated lower indicates that the "glossiness" factor remained fairly constant between the two groups. Thus, in this arena at least, there appeared to be little incentive to inordinately polish the products of teaching and learning. It is important to keep in mind, though, that the construction of portfolios in this study took place in a low-stakes setting. When the rewards are more substantial, the impulse to "dress up" the portfolio will no doubt be much greater.

> There appeared to be little incentive to inordinately polish the products of teaching and learning.

7. *How should the portfolio entries be structured?* Once we had identified the areas to be documented and had made some decisions about the general form and content of the portfolio, the next step was to develop specifications and instructions for each portfolio entry.

In our early discussions, we debated whether the portfolio task should be tightly structured or more open-ended. Should we fully specify the methods and materials for each entry or let the teachers themselves decide how best to demonstrate competence?

We weighed the benefits and drawbacks of both the structured and the open-ended approaches. Previous efforts at using portfolios to assess teachers in licensure and career ladder programs in Tennessee and Florida revealed that, if the portfolio task is too open-ended or ill-defined, the task can easily turn into a paper chase. The portfolios that teachers submitted in these previous ventures were unmanageably large and unfocused. With this in mind, we knew that we wanted more than a container filled with whatever the teacher felt was appropriate. On the other hand, we were concerned that the more we defined and constrained the task of documentation, the greater the risk of excluding the many (and unexpected) forms that exemplary teaching can take.

We ultimately decided that the best approach was to be explicit and directive about the form and procedure of documentation but permissive about the content of the portfolio, giving teachers as much latitude as possible to make decisions about their teaching.[12]

> It is important to ask what minimum number of assessment center exercises or portfolio entries are required to determine a teacher's competence.

The initial feedback from teachers participating in the field test was clear: they wanted even more direction. Responding to this request in the next version of their "Portfolio Construction Kit," the biology team provided step-by-step instructions for the teachers to follow. As more portfolios are completed, however, and numerous and diverse models for documenting exemplary practice are available for teachers to review, many questions about instructions and procedures will fade away.

8. *How much evidence is it necessary to include in a portfolio?* Given that performance-based exercises are costly to develop and administer and that portfolios are time-consuming to prepare and expensive to score, it is important to ask what minimum number of assessment center exercises or portfolio entries are required to determine a teacher's competence. Are 10 portfolio entries enough? Are two too few? Edward Haertel, an associate director of the project, sees it as a question of the "value added" by each additional entry.[13] If we were forced to make a decision about a teacher's competence based on a single portfolio entry or assessment center or exercise, what would a second entry or exercise add to this judgment? What would a third contribute?

In part, the question can be answered by tying it to the number of critical teaching tasks identified. In biology, the development team identified four broad areas: planning, instruction, evaluation, and professional growth. By sampling performances within each area through a variety of assessment approaches (i.e., assessment center exercises, portfolios, classroom observations, and written tests), we can begin to set boundaries on the amount of evidence that might be necessary to obtain a reasonably comprehensive picture of a teacher's knowledge and skills.

Interestingly, after completing their portfolios, the biology teachers argued that, rather than submit a videotape of a lesson from one instructional unit, and a lesson plan from still another, they should draw all their portfolio entries from the same four- to six-week unit on a single topic. They felt that this method would make their task more coherent and manageable.

The way we dealt with the matter of how much evidence is necessary was determined by real-world constraints.

But a counterargument is that evidence collected from different teaching activities across different topics provides multiple windows on a teacher's knowledge and skill. For example, a lesson plan on ecology presents one view of a teacher's subject-matter knowledge, while the same teacher's evaluation of student papers from a unit on genetics reveals that teacher's knowledge in a different area of the curriculum. These multiple views also make it easier to detect the "one-lesson wonder"— the teacher who pulls out the same stellar lesson during the principal's once-a-year observation but has little else to offer. In addition, requiring all of a teacher's documentation to come from a single four- to six-week period would probably place so much pressure on the teachers that teaching and learning might be seriously undermined during that time.

Ideally, we sought to develop portfolio entries that were manageable as well as meaningful to both those constructing them and those evaluating them. Ultimately, the way we dealt with the matter of how much evidence is necessary was determined by real-world constraints. Given that the teachers in this study were constructing portfolios in addition to carrying out their regular teaching duties, we were concerned that the task be one that they could be expected to complete. We aimed at collecting just enough evidence to allow us to make some reasonable judgments about a teacher's knowledge and skills and to explore the effectiveness of portfolios as a strategy for assessing teachers.

According to the feedback from the elementary literacy teachers, our demands on them were unrealistic. Completing a full set of portfolio entries in one school year was too taxing. Even though we designed the portfolios to capture much of what routinely takes place in classrooms, completing them required more than assembling the products of classroom life. In particular, writing the reflective statements and captioning the contents of the portfolio took a substantial amount of time.

Should the portfolio display all of a person's work—the good, the bad, and the ugly—or only the work of which the person is most proud?

The one-year limit, imposed because of research constraints, is somewhat artificial, however. In actual practice, teachers are likely to take several years to prepare their portfolios, possibly beginning during their undergraduate years. This longer time frame will allow for a varied pace to suit individual needs and interests and will provide teachers with adequate time to receive support and feedback on their portfolios and teaching.

9. *Should a portfolio represent a teacher's best work?* Tom Bird, a member of the TAP staff, offers various images of a "portfolio"—an artist's portfolio, a pilot's log, a salesperson's catalogue, a scout's merit badge sash—each of which presents the owner's work in dramatically different ways.[14] But which model is most appropriate for teaching? Should the school-teacher's portfolio resemble the photographer's, which presents only the very best work, or the pilot's log, in which every flight is recorded? Should the portfolio display all of a person's work—the good, the bad, and the ugly—or only the work of which the person is most proud? Or is teaching so dissimilar from other occupations that the model for the school-teacher's portfolio should not be borrowed from any of the existing models?

We took the view that a portfolio should contain the teacher's very best work. We expected that, in constructing a portfolio, a teacher would have ample opportunity to collect work samples over an extended period of time and to select work that most flatteringly illustrated his or her knowledge and accomplishments. A lesson that flopped, for example, would not be documented in the portfolio—unless it contributed in some significant way to the teacher's or students' growth or revealed important insights about the class or course. But, while we expected the portfolio to portray a teacher's best work, we also took the view that the unnecessary lamination of the genuine products of teaching was as unseemly as "a carpenter . . . bronz[ing] her tools."[15]

> Some project members raised the concern that if we focused on best teaching, everyone's portfolio would look alike.

In actuality, given the pace of the project, the teachers often had little opportunity to select from various samples of their work. For example, during the designated time period, the biology teachers taught only one or two lessons that provided evidence of their use of alternative materials. Thus many teachers submitted their only attempt. In this case, the teachers felt constraints imposed by the project prevented them from demonstrating their best teaching. Presumably, when the process of constructing and revising a portfolio is allowed to evolve over a longer time span, the portfolios should contain teachers' best attempts at responding to the complex problems of teaching.

Some project members raised the concern that if we focused on best teaching, everyone's portfolio would look alike. Given sufficient time, wouldn't all teachers be able to present exemplary portfolios? The portfolios we reviewed provided evidence to the contrary. We found considerable variation in what teachers view as their best efforts. In some instances, teachers passionately defend practices that most of their colleagues would find unacceptable. In addition, not all teachers are equally able to step back and see whether their own instruction does, in fact, reflect the conception of teaching they espouse.

10. *Should a portfolio be a solo performance?* Consider the following two models for portfolio construction. In the "solo" model, teachers are expected to complete their portfolios without the assistance of others. In the "collaborative" model, teachers are directed to seek the participation of others in developing their portfolios. In the first model, collaboration is treated as cheating; in the second, teachers are encouraged to work together.

One of the drawbacks of using portfolios for evaluation is the difficulty of ensuring that the work presented is entirely that of the person whose name is on the folder. But this potential stumbling block can be turned into a stepping stone: treat collaboration as a virtue.[16] In this view, teachers would be expected to seek out the assistance of others in their teaching and in the construction of their portfolios.

Teachers tend to work in isolation, and the few interactions that do occur between colleagues are likely to involve nonacademic concerns rather than substantive issues of curriculum or instruction.[17] If one outcome of portfolio assessment is to promote a culture of collaboration among teachers, then a significant contribution will have been made to the profession.

In a program of teacher assessment that blends a variety of approaches, there are multiple opportunities for cross-checks.

With the collaborative model, the person whose name is on the portfolio is still responsible for mastery of the knowledge and skills displayed in it, but what distinguishes this situation from the solo model is how the teacher achieves that mastery. A doctoral dissertation, for example, is a coached performance, but the student is ultimately responsible for both the final product and mastery of the subject matter.[18] The end result is that the doctoral student—or classroom teacher—is able to achieve a greater understanding by working with others than by working alone.

While the problem of establishing authorship is not entirely eliminated with the collaborative model, it is significantly less important. And, in a program of teacher assessment that blends a variety of approaches, there are multiple opportunities for cross-checks—through assessment center exercises, classroom observations, attestations by colleagues, written tests, and follow-up interviews after a teacher has submitted a portfolio—to ensure that the portfolio truly represents the teacher's talents and accomplishments.

Collaboration is not without risk, however. Without supports and guidelines in place, it can become an empty ritual rather than an opportunity for fruitful professional exchange.

Even worse, if collaboration is not voluntary and takes place in a high-stakes environment, the pressure of working together could tear people apart. One way to reduce the likelihood that collaboration will turn into conflict is to ensure that mentors and colleagues assisting a teacher play only a supportive role. Portfolio collaborators, in this view, are advocates for the teacher, not evaluators. Only later, after the collaboration has taken place, is the completed portfolio evaluated.

> "Professional judgment" may be the key to portfolio evaluation, but simply conjuring up the words does not solve the problem.

11. *How should a portfolio be evaluated?* Developing procedures for constructing a portfolio poses one set of puzzles; evaluating portfolios, another. Not only does a portfolio contain much more information than is normally available for assessing a teacher's competence, but also its contents have been customized by each teacher to fit his or her personal teaching style and context. Each teacher's portfolio is unique.

After exploring the virtues and difficulties of using a fine-grain, analytic scoring scheme to evaluate assessment center performances in the first phase of the project, we opted for an entirely different approach to evaluating portfolios.[19] Rather than take a teacher's portfolio apart for a point-by-point analysis, we believed that a portfolio is more coherent and informative when evaluated holistically. This approach depends heavily on "professional judgment," a critical component of evaluation in many professions. In exercising professional judgment, one brings to bear knowledge of a given profession's practices and traditions.

"Professional judgment" may be the key to portfolio evaluation, but simply conjuring up the words does not solve the problem. In order for people to exercise such judgment in a disciplined manner, they need to be very clear about the performance criteria. Without some kind of structure or guidelines, people tend to go to one extreme or the other—either they retreat to unsubstantiated global impressions based on first reactions or gut feelings, or they try to simplify the assessment task by looking for specific, objective criteria and become overly narrow in their evaluation. The difficult task is to steer the middle course and make only supported judgments about specific aspects of the problem being evaluated without reducing the judgment task to a formula.[20]

We aimed at achieving this objective by having trained examiners, experienced and knowledgeable in the content area and grade level, rate each portfolio entry according to a few broad but specific criteria. In this case, the criteria that we applied came from a draft of standards from the National Board for Professional Teaching Standards: board-certified teachers (1) are committed to students and their learning, (2) know their subject matters and how to teach them, (3) manage and monitor student learning, (4) think about and learn from practice, and (5) participate in learning communities.[21]

> In scoring the portfolios, each entry, as well as a candidate's overall performance, was rated for each appropriate standard on a five-point scale.

We modified the language of the standards to better suit the purposes of the field test and added a paragraph describing each standard in greater detail to help the examiners more fully grasp its meaning. The standards and descriptive paragraphs were broad enough to guide the examiners but not so specific as to make their task mechanical. Given that the standards were released well after the development of the portfolio entries, however, the match between the two was not always perfect. Nevertheless, the fit was good enough to simulate a process that the board might follow in certifying teachers.

In scoring the portfolios, each entry, as well as a candidate's overall performance, was rated for each appropriate standard on a five-point scale: unacceptable, weak, adequate, proficient, and superb. Each scale point was accompanied by a paragraph describing the main features of a performance at that level. In our simulation, the line between adequate and proficient marked the difference between a respectable performance and a board-certified one.

We employed a two-stage procedure in scoring the portfolios. First, small groups of examiners were trained to rate specific portfolio entries, and they scored only those entries. Second, caucus groups were formed, with each group composed of members from the different examining teams. The caucus groups were assigned the task of looking across all of the performances of several candidates and making final recommendations for board certification. In this way, the scoring represented an amalgam of judgments from different raters and different vantage points. Through this process, we aimed to allow the examiners to apply their professional judgment, but we offset their subjectivity through training and multiple independent ratings.[22]

> **Through portfolios, teaching and learning can be seen as they unfold and extend over time.**

12. *What does a portfolio contribute that can't be achieved through other methods of teacher assessment?* Portfolios are messy, time-consuming to construct, cumbersome to store, and costly to evaluate. Are they worth the trouble? Why do we even need them?

Portfolios enable teachers to document their teaching in an authentic setting and to bring in the context of their own classrooms in a way that no other form of assessment can. Classroom observations allow teaching to be seen in context, but observations, which tend to take place only a few times a year, are isolated snapshots, disconnected from the events that preceded or followed the observed lesson. Through portfolios, teaching and learning can be seen as they unfold and extend over time. And when the actual artifacts of teaching are combined with a teacher's reflections, portfolios permit us to look beneath the surface of the performance itself and examine the decisions that shaped a teacher's actions.

Along with assessment center exercises, (improved) written tests, and direct observations, portfolios can contribute valuable evidence about a teacher's pedagogical capacities. However, as Shulman points out, "Each of these several approaches to the assessment of teachers is, in itself, as fundamentally flawed as it is reasonably suitable, as perilously insufficient as it is peculiarly fitting."[23] Written tests permit broad sampling of a teacher's subject-matter competence but are remote from the complexities of practice. Assessment center exercises enable teachers to demonstrate their skills and knowledge through a series of realistic simulations in standardized setting but are not connected to an actual context. Direct observations allow teaching to be seen in its full complexity, but the rating scales used in observations fail to tap many of teaching's critical dimensions. Portfolios are flawed as well, but no other method of assessment can equal them in providing a connection to the contexts and personal histories of real teaching.

While this research took place without real-world incentives and consequences pressing on the process of building and evaluating portfolios, we were largely satisfied with the final results. The teachers felt that their portfolios accurately reflected what took place in their classrooms. The development teams who designed the portfolios felt that the porfolios captured what they were intended to capture. Those evaluating the portfolios felt that the complexities and contexts of real teaching came through. Most important, we found that portfolios are possible—not an insignificant claim, given the results of previous efforts at portfolio assessment.

This research focused on the evaluative function of portfolios. But portfolios can serve a formative function as well. In fact, while they have an indispensable role to play in the evaluation of teachers' pedagogical competence, their larger contribution may lie in the ways that they can reshape the profession of teaching. Portfolios can give teachers a purpose and framework for preserving and sharing their work, provide occasions for mentoring and collegial interactions, and stimulate teachers to reflect on their own work and on the act of teaching. However, if completed in a perfunctory fashion, portfolios can also become nothing more than another obstacle to good teaching. As Bird observes, "The potential of portfolio procedures depends as much on the political, organizational, and professional settings in which they are used as on anything about the procedures themselves."[24] Our original problem in this research was to generate a prototype—to "grow" portfolios. In this we succeeded. What remains is to consider the ways that institutional and professional forces will support or subvert the promise of portfolios.

REFERENCES AND NOTES

1. The research reported here was supported by a grant from the Carnegie Corporation of New York. The opinions expressed are those of the author and in no way reflect the views of that organization. Moreover, while this work was carried out in the interests of the National Board for Professional Teaching Standards, the board is proceeding with its own extensive research program and will not necessarily adopt the model described here.

2. Lee Shulman, "Assessment for Teaching: An Initiative for the Profession," *Phi Delta Kappan,* September 1987, pp. 38–44; and idem, "The Paradox of Teacher Assessment," in *New Directions for Teacher Assessment* (Princeton, N.J.: Educational Testing Service, 1989), pp. 13–27.

3. Lee Shulman, "A Union of Insufficiencies: Strategies for Teacher Assessment in a Period of Educational Reform," *Educational Leadership,* November 1988, pp. 36–41.

4. Lee Shulman, Tom Bird, and Edward Haertel, *Toward Alternative Assessments of Teaching: A Report of Work in Progress* (Stanford, Calif.: Teacher Assessment Project, Stanford University, 1989).

5. Bruce King, *Thinking About Linking Portfolios with Assessment Center Exercises: Examples from the Teacher Assessment Project* (Stanford, Calif.: Teacher Assessment Project, Stanford University, 1990); and Linda Vavrus and Angelo Collins, "Portfolio Documentation and Assessment Center Exercises: A Marriage Made for Teacher Assessment," *Teacher Education Quarterly,* forthcoming.

6. Susan Stodolsky, *The Subject Matters* (Chicago: University of Chicago Press, 1988).

7. Sheila Valencia, William McGinley, and P. David Pearson, "Assessing Reading and Writing: Building a More Complete Picture," in Gerald Duffy, ed., *Reading in the Middle School,* 2nd ed. (Newark, Del.: International Reading Association, 1990), pp. 124–46.

8. Shulman, "A Union of Insufficiencies," p. 40.

9. Ibid.

10. Philip Jackson, *Life in Classrooms* (New York: Holt, Rinehart & Winston, 1968); and Seymour Sarason, *The Culture of the School and the Problem of Change,* 2nd ed. (Boston: Allyn and Bacon, 1982).

11. Angelo Collins, *The BioTAP Story: A Narrative Description of an Exploration* (Stanford, Calif.: Teacher Assessment Project, Stanford University, 1990).

12. Tom Bird, personal correspondence, 13 March 1990.

13. Edward Haertel, personal communication, 20 November 1989.

14. Tom Bird, "The Schoolteacher's Portfolio: An Essay on Possibilities," in Jason Millman and Linda Darling-Hammond, eds., *The New Handbook of Teacher Evaluation: Assessing Elementary and Secondary School Teachers,* 2nd ed. (Newbury Park, Calif.: Sage, 1990), pp. 241–56.

15. Ibid., p. 242.

16. Shulman, "A Union of Insufficiencies."

17. Dan Lortie, *Schoolteacher: A Sociological Study* (Chicago: University of Chicago Press, 1975).

18. Shulman, "A Union of Insufficiencies."

19. Deborah Kerdeman, *The 100 Statements Project: A Study in the Dynamics of Teacher Assessment* (Stanford, Calif.: Teacher Assessment Project, Stanford University, 1989).

20. Edward Haertel, "From Expert Opinions to Reliable Scores: Psychometrics for Judgment-Based Teacher Assessment," paper presented at the annual meeting of the American Educational Research Association, Boston, 1990.

21. *Toward High and Rigorous Standards for the Teaching Profession* (Washington, D.C.: National Board for Professional Teaching Standards, 1989).

22. Tom Bird, *Report on the Rating Procedure Used to Assess Portfolios and Assessment Center Exercises for High School Biology Teachers* (Stanford, Calif.: Teacher Assessment Project, Stanford University, 1990).

23. Shulman, "A Union of Insufficiencies," p. 38.

24. Bird, *Report on the Rating Procedure,* p. 241.

Using Portfolios to Evaluate Teachers: Learning from Ourselves

by Christine Hult

F or evaluating writing, portfolios have been touted as an assessment method with advantages over other methods; portfolios allow teachers a window on a writer's work in process, and they allow writers the opportunity to reflect on their own work (Larsen; Belanoff and Elbow). Portfolios have also been adapted for the evaluation of teachers and their teaching. In a recent American Association for Higher Education publication (Edgerton, et al.), the authors describe how teachers can develop a written record of their teaching through assembling a teaching portfolio. Just as the teacher evaluation process parallels in many ways the evaluation of writing, so the teaching portfolio can be seen as parallel to the writing portfolio. In this article, I will explore how what we have learned from writing portfolios can help us to design teacher evaluations using teaching portfolios.

Mary Ellen Weimer in her book *Improving College Teaching* emphasizes that if teacher improvement is the desired outcome of a teacher evaluation program, teachers must voluntarily participate in the process. We know this with our writing students; we can make suggestions for revisions, but unless they truly want to improve a piece of writing, nothing we say will matter. All teachers should be invited to participate in any teacher evaluation program, but each teacher should be put in charge of his or her own instructional improvement plan. Indi-

From *Journal of Teaching Writing*, vol. 12, no. 1, 1993, pp. 57–66. © 1993 by Christine Hult. Reprinted with permission.

viduals should decide the extent of the changes and the means employed to accomplish the changes. The evaluator, then, serves as a resource person, just as the writing teacher serves as a resource person, making suggestions for change but ultimately allowing the student, or in this case the teacher, ownership of his or her own improvement process. When we are working closely with teachers in a coach-improver role, we see them weaving a "text" of their own teaching, just as we see writers weave a text as we coach them through subsequent drafts. A teacher's woven "text" can be captured in the form of a teaching portfolio.

A teacher's woven "text" can be captured in the form of a teaching portfolio.

Portfolios seek to capture the complexity of teaching and writing and, furthermore, to encourage the portfolio's compiler to self-reflect on the meaning of its content. The AAHE document calls this "reflective practice," the necessary precursor of improvement. They do, however, point out as well that we need to carefully determine the needs and purposes for teaching portfolios: needs which range from "evaluating a candidate for promotion and tenure to facilitating good conversation about teaching" (7). Once we have determined our purposes, then decisions about format and content of the portfolio can follow.

Edward Kearns points out this same confusion of purposes in writing portfolio assessment. If our purpose is to assess writing competency, say Kearns, it makes sense to establish appropriate criteria and to assess whether or not students are able to meet those criteria: "the question of a student's 'best' writing is irrelevant" (51) in competency assessments. If, on the other hand, our assessment purpose is for placement of students into appropriate courses, "then we wish not only to exempt some students from unnecessary course work, but also to direct others toward needed courses and services" (51). Kearns points out that for placement purposes what we need are representative rather than best writing samples. In his article, Kearns argues that writing portfolios serve neither the competence nor the representative assessment purposes; rather, they fulfill a third purpose or goal: "to help students become independent and personally empowered" (52) writers.

Similarly, we often have a confusion of purposes when assessing teachers. What are our reasons for evaluating teachers anyway? What do we hope to accomplish? Two related but conflicting goals underlie most teacher evaluation: one is the goal of accountability (achieved through summative evaluations of performance); the other is the goal of improvement in classroom teaching and learning (achieved through formative evaluations of performance). Too often in teacher evaluation, the two goals are conflated.

> **What are our reasons for evaluating teachers anyway? What do we hope to accomplish?**

To illustrate this confusion of purposes, I would like to recount an incident that occurred at the Breckenridge WPA conference in the summer of 1992. One of the keynote speakers was Pat Hutchings, who has done considerable work with teaching portfolios in conjunction with the AAHE's teaching initiative. Pat asked the conference audience whether any of them had used teaching portfolios at their schools. I was very surprised when no one from the contingent who teach writing at a large research university raised her hand. I was under the impression, from conversations with the writing program director, that this particular university used teaching portfolios extensively when evaluating writing faculty. In later conversations with some of those writing faculty, I discovered that what the director called "teaching portfolios" the writing faculty called "tenure dossiers." The writing faculty did not consider these dossiers as teaching portfolios at all because their purpose was to document their own teaching abilities for tenure and promotion decision-making (a summative purpose) rather than for improvement of teaching (a formative purpose).

The terms formative and summative evaluation were introduced by Michael Scriven in a 1967 AERA monograph (as cited in the *American Educators' Encyclopedia*). Formative evaluation is defined as "assessment that takes place during the developmental (formative) stages of a program or a product" (226). Information gathered during a formative assessment "may then be used to alter a program, to revise materials, to restructure a program design, or to reconsider goals and objectives" (226).

In contrast, summative evaluation is defined as "the assessment of the overall effectiveness of a program or a product. Unlike formative evaluation, which is carried out during the development of a program, summative evaluation takes place after a program is fully developed and implemented" (551). The encyclopedia points out that "the results of summative evaluations usually are a major concern for policy makers, and the results of formative evaluations are of particular interest to . . . those working in the program" (552).

As I am using these terms, formative evaluation of teachers occurs as they are teaching and is designed to provide information that may help them to alter their teaching in ways that improve student learning; similarly formative evaluations of writers occur as they are drafting, often through peer or teacher conferencing, and are designed to help the writer improve a particular piece. In contrast, summative evaluations of teachers occur as a one-time assessment to judge overall teaching performance with the purpose of "summing up" the effectiveness of that performance, usually as a way to guide administrators in personnel decisions. Similarly, summative evaluation of writing occurs when the student turns in a finished product and the teacher evaluates it for a grade. Most assessment instruments, and the resultant data, including portfolios, can be used for either formative or summative evaluation purposes.

> Most assessment instruments, including portfolios, can be used for either formative or summative evaluation purposes.

Too often in portfolio assessments, because the formative is not separated from the summative, the two goals of accountability and improvement are used as though interchangeable when in fact they may not even be compatible. For example, a summative performance review of the dossier of a teacher who has received numerous complaints may have as its purpose the documenting of that teacher's inadequacies for purposes of terminating his or her employment. We shouldn't delude ourselves into thinking that such an evaluation is meant to help the teacher improve. On the other hand, a formative evaluation using a teaching portfolio is intended to provide the teacher with valuable feedback that can be used in self-improvement efforts. In formative evaluations, one gets another chance, an opportunity to "revise" one's performance. And a serious effort at formative evaluation may mitigate the necessity for extensive summative evaluation, because the evaluator is able to see the shaping of a teacher or a writer over time in a rich and varied context.

I would like to turn now to a discussion of the formative uses of portfolios, with the attendant goals of teacher and writer improvement. Bonnie Sunstein, in her introduction to the collection *Portfolio Portraits,* says that "Portfolios mean more than evaluation or assessment. They are tied to our definition of literacy. When we read and write constantly, when we reflect on who we are and who we want to be, we cannot help but grow. Over time, portfolios help us identify and organize the specifics of our reading and writing. They catalogue our accomplishments and goals, from successes to instructive failures . . . We need to allow portfolios some growing and breathing space before we freeze them into a definition or a standardized mandate" (xii). Although Sunstein was speaking specifically of writing portfolios, I would argue for giving teaching portfolios similar growing time and breathing space before using them summatively in what Pat Hutchings calls high-stakes employment decisions.

Because of the similarities between teaching and writing portfolios, it is instructive to apply some of what we have learned about effective practice with writing portfolios to teaching portfolios. Donald Graves in Chapter 1 of *Portfolio Portraits* outlines "seven principles to insure growth" when using portfolios. Each of Graves' principles can be constructively applied to formative uses of teaching portfolios as well.

1. INVOLVE THE [TEACHERS] BEING EVALUATED

> The portfolio movement promises one of the best opportunities for students to learn how to examine their own work and participate in the entire literacy/learning process (4).

When we evaluate teachers, we have typically approached it the same way that we have approached evaluating students—top down. We know from Weimer and others that teacher improvement will occur only when the teachers are not only involved in the process but also ultimately have control over their own improvement agendas. Weimer points out that faculty often resist efforts at instructional improvement, especially when they are imposed from "above." First, faculty feel threatened because the "need to improve implies incompetence in professional arenas where they see themselves as experts" (17). Second,

> **Faculty often resist efforts at instructional improvement, especially when they are imposed from "above."**

they feel threatened because attention to their teaching makes them feel personally vulnerable and open to scrutiny and criticism. Sometimes faculty resistance can be overcome in the context of support for any and all efforts to improve, but it would be naive to suppose that all faculty will cheerfully sign on.

Just as students need to be encouraged to reflect on their writing and learning, teachers need to be encouraged to reflect on their teaching. A number of methods are helpful to faculty, everything from peer coaching programs to master teacher mentoring programs, to videotaping and self-critique, to teaching portfolios. The literature suggests that one of the main problems with efforts to improve teaching is the breakdown between ideas learned by faculty at workshops and seminars and the actual implementation of these ideas in the classroom. I would venture to guess that a similar breakdown might occur once a teaching portfolio has been developed. We need to work toward a cycle of learning, self-reflection, and performance feedback for improvement actually to take hold in the classroom.

2. HELP THE STAFF KEEP PORTFOLIOS OF THEIR OWN

> Professionals engaged in portfolio study [who have not kept portfolios themselves] are not unlike professionals who teach writing without writing themselves (5).

Administrators who are in the role of evaluating teachers should be encouraged to keep portfolios of "reflective practice" on their own work. In this way, we can all become better at explaining our work to ourselves and to others. Administrators, myself included, are notoriously devoid of reflective practice. We also have a hard time explaining our administrative work—for example, where is the evidence for what I do as a WPA and as an Assistant Department Head? The AAHE document suggests that what should be included in a portfolio are samples of actual work: "syllabi, daily assignments, special reading lists, laboratory exercises, student papers, student examiniations . . . all the ARTIFACTS of teaching" (9). What are the artifacts of an administrator? Reports, memos, proposals, curricular outlines, all the daily writing that administrators produce while about their business. A portfolio reflecting on such artifacts could help to document an administrator's otherwise "invisible" work.

3.   BROADEN THE PURPOSE OF PORTFOLIOS

> I had found that portfolios caused people to experiment, though I was not sure why (6).

If evaluation typically does one thing, it is to kill experimentation and creativity. Think about the times when you have been evaluated; if you're like me, you chose the tried and true, not the innovative and imaginative. In connection with a faculty review, I was recently observed in the classroom by the academic Dean of my college. Once I knew that he was coming to observe, I made certain that I would be "teaching" that day, so there would be something for him to watch. I had to drag out a lesson which I had used successfully before, even though it was not totally relevant to the research writing class I was currently teaching. Because I teach writing, many of my class periods are taken up by peer group work, student oral reports or readings of works-in-progress, activities that require my behind-the-scenes orchestration, but may look to the uninitiated as though I'm not really teaching.

In contrast, using a portfolio as the ongoing site of reflective practice can promote rather than stifle creativity. In a portfolio, I would discuss my attempts at innovation and how they were working with my students. I could show the constant adjustments that must take place when a teacher is sensitive to both the needs of the students and the demands of the subject. As well as including the products of good teaching (syllabi, course outlines, student creative work, etc.), the AAHE document suggests that portfolios should include material from oneself: "descriptive material on current and recent teaching responsibilities and practices . . . Descriptions of steps taken to evaluate and improve one's teaching" (8). By reflecting on our practice, we can enhance our creativity.

4.   KEEP INSTRUCTIONAL OPPORTUNITIES OPEN

> Make your portfolio a collection of all different kinds of things you've learned . . . In this way a portfolio provides a history of learning (9).

Teachers and administrators should take a similar approach to documenting a history of their own learning about what they do. They shouldn't cut off non-academic areas of their lives, but use their learning in all spheres to inform their practice. Active, alive teachers are active, alive people. They are in tune with their political and social context; they are avid readers who follow current affairs with interest, often becoming passionately involved with causes. One of our teachers ran the campaign of a local politician, another is active in women's health issues, a third in environmental causes, and so on. Rather than compartmentalizing their lives into "academic" and "private" selves, teachers should be encouraged to bring their life-long learning to bear in the classroom. Portfolios should include information from others as well as from ourselves: students, colleagues, and others, such as parents, employers, or community members who come to us because of our reputation or expertise (Edgerton 8). All can provide evidence of our effectiveness as educators.

5.   REEXAMINE ISSUES IN COMPARABILITY

> Most evaluation structures do not inform teaching. Rather than set benchmarks, research ought to reveal potential for more effective teaching and learning (10).

The same issues of comparability in writing portfolios are present in teaching portfolios. How do we compare portfolios of a literacy critic with a Writing Program Administrator, for example? I would urge that we not mandate teaching portfolios in promotion and tenure decisions until we have done a better job of solving the reliability problems that confound summative uses of portfolios. Rather, all teachers could be encouraged to keep a teaching record wherein they reflect on their classroom endeavors. As one who serves on such promotion and tenure committees, I have found most useful those self-reflective pieces that discuss a teacher's attempts at innovation and reactions to how new ideas "worked" in the classroom. Student evaluations can provide the motivation for a teacher's dialogue with herself about how students perceived the teacher's efforts and subsequent plans to adapt less-successful methods. But the very process of assembling and reflecting upon teaching portfolios goes a long way toward helping teachers improve because "they enable faculty—indeed REQUIRE them—to become more important actors in monitoring and evaluating the quality of their own work" (Edgerton 5).

6. STUDY THE EFFECT OF SCHOOL POLICY ON PORTFOLIO PRACTICE

> Perhaps we ought to consider policy as a reflection of what works. For those teachers and students who demonstrate effective work in the classroom with portfolios, a process of gradual expansion might be considered until policy becomes a reflection of what is already working (11).

We need to take a go-slow approach; as Sunstein suggests, let's look at what we're doing with portfolios, but let's allow portfolios time to blossom rather than make their use a rigid formula. At our university, we are encouraging teachers who are tenure-track to begin writing down their thoughts about their teaching in a "teaching log," which may or may not be included in a tenure dossier. However, such logs are extremely helpful for tenure committees who have a chance through reading them to overhear a teacher's conversations with herself regarding teaching. This process is analogous to the writing teacher being allowed via the writing portfolio to overhear a writer thinking through his or her learning processes.

7. ENLIST THE INGENUITY OF TEACHERS

> Teachers, more than professors, administrators, or policy makers, will determine the success of portfolio practice (12).

Encourage and support any efforts by both teachers and writers to improve what they are doing. Evaluators can make suggestions, but the "ingenuity" of those developing the portfolios should be allowed free rein. Evaluating teachers is an enormously complex task with competing purposes, goals, and methods. We need to view teaching as a complicated, expressive, human activity deserving of a sympathetic, thoughtful, flexible response.

Deborah Tannen, in her book *You Just Don't Understand: Women and Men in Conversation,* cites a small survey conducted by *The Chronicle of Higher Education* that asked six university professors why they had chosen academic careers. The two women in the survey both answered that they went into academe because of a desire to teach. The four men answered that the independence and freedom afforded them in an academic profession was their primary motivation. Tannen uses this survey as evidence that the women focused on connection to students as their primary motivation, whereas the men focused on their freedom from others' control (43). Putting the gender differences aside, both perspectives are right. Teachers want the freedom and independence to be able to influence positively their students' learning. Portfolios, used formatively, can help with this goal.

WORKS CITED

American Educators' Encyclopedia, Rev. ed. Eds. Edward L. Dejnozka and David E. Kapel. New York: Greenwood Press, 1990, 226; 551–552.

Belanoff, Pat, and Peter Elbow. "Using Portfolios to Increase Collaboration and Community in a Writing Program." *WPA: Writing Program Administration* 9,3 (1986): 27–39.

Edgerton, Russell, Patricia Hutchings, and Kathleen Quinlan. *The Teaching Portfolio: Capturing the Scholarship in Teaching.* Washington, D.C.: American Association of Higher Education, 1992.

Graves, Donald H., and Bonnie S. Sunstein, Eds. *Portfolio Portraits.* Portsmouth, N.H.: Heinemann, 1992.

Kearns, Edward. "On the Running Board of the Portfolio Bandwagon." *WPA Writing Program Administration* 16,3 (1993): 50–58.

Larsen, Richard L. "Using Portfolios in the Assessment of Writing in the Academic Disciplines." *Portfolios: Process and Product.* Ed. Pat Belanoff and Marcia Dickson. Portsmouth: Boynton/Cook, 1991, 137–150.

Tannen, Deborah. *You Just Don't Understand: Women and Men in Conversation.* New York: Ballantine, 1990.

Weimer, Maryellen. *Improving College Teaching.* San Francisco: Jossey-Bass, 1990.

Integrated Portfolios as Tools for Differentiated Teacher Evaluation: A Proposal

by Helen B. Regan

The public's interest in and the teacher's need for extensive scrutiny is far more intense for beginning teachers than it is for experienced teachers. While most experienced teachers can be relied on to perform at least satisfactorily, the competence of beginning teachers has not yet been demonstrated. (See Regan, Anctil, Dubea, Hofmann, and Vaillancourt, 1992.) This difference in the reasons for evaluating novice and experienced teachers and this difference in the type of information needed about the performance of each group, has implications for teacher-evaluation systems. For novice teachers, evaluations should emphasize accountability, but for experienced teachers whose fundamental competence has been established, evaluations should more properly emphasize professional development.

Current teacher-evaluation systems do not meaningfully distinguish between these two groups of teachers; most commonly, existing systems respond quantitatively to the different purposes for evaluating beginning and experienced teachers by requiring more frequent classroom observations of beginning teachers. However, existing systems do not discriminate in what is looked for during the observations nor do they differentiate between the need for detailed accountability of performance for novice teachers or the need to stimulate professional develop-

From *Journal of Personnel Evaluation in Education,* vol. 7, no. 4, December 1993, pp. 275–90. © 1993 by Kluwer Academic Publishers—Boston. Reprinted with permission.

ment for experienced teachers. This practice exists despite literature documenting substantial differences in the performance of novice, experienced, and expert teachers (Anctil, 1990; Berliner, 1986).

In addition to the failure to distinguish between novice and experienced teachers, current teacher-evaluation practice also makes unrealistic demands on administrators' time. Forced to choose where to spend limited time, many administrators make the rational decision to devote their energies to beginners and other teachers whose competence is in question. The vast majority of teachers are left without any meaningful contact with either administrators or other teachers; they are neither held accountable in any real way nor helped to develop professionally through interaction with colleagues. Current practices serve neither the novice nor the experienced teacher to any meaningful extent.

> Current teacher-evaluation practice makes unrealistic demands on administrators' time.

Finally, most current teacher-evaluation systems examine only general pedagogical knowledge (Millman and Darling-Hammond, 1990; Schwab, 1990). Evaluation tools that reveal teacher thinking and that make a direct link between teaching and learning remain a hope for the future (Costa, Garmston & Lambert, 1988).

Experimentation with portfolios as tools to assess both teacher and student performance is currently occurring around the country (Wolf, 1991; Bird, 1990). This article proposes the use of integrated portfolios that connect student performance with specific teaching events as a teacher-evaluation tool capable of applying rigorous and substantive(but appropriately different) standards to both novice and experienced teachers. The use of two types of integrated portfolios establishes detailed accountability for novice teachers as well as offering the possibility for professional development, and for experienced teachers it stimulates deep and meaningful professional development while maintaining a level of accountability. The differentiation between the two groups of teachers allocates administrator time reasonably, draws in specialists now usually excluded from the evaluation process, and creates a stimulating forum for accountability and professional development. Finally, both integrated portfolios capture teacher thinking as well as teacher performance, and link them explicitly to student learning, which brings a more sophisticated and substantive dimension to teacher evaluation.

The following sections describe the two types of integrated portfolios, suggest procedures for their review, and illustrate each type using my recent experience teaching a high-school chemistry class.

> Taken as a unit, the integrated portfolios tell a coherent story about the relationship between the teacher's work and the student's learning.

INTEGRATED PORTFOLIOS

Integrated portfolios capture the complexities of teaching (as do all good teacher portfolios). However, instead of being organized around discrete teaching tasks, the teaching entries in integrated portfolios have immediate relationship to intended student outcome. Likewise, the student entries in an integrated portfolio demonstrate the extent and quality of student learning for a particular outcome. Taken as a unit, the integrated portfolios tell a coherent story about the relationship between the teacher's work and the student's learning.

Integrated portfolios combine teacher and student work around a large concept of fundamental skill and formulate a student outcome. The portfolio includes artifacts of teaching such as videotapes or audiotapes of lessons, teaching materials, teacher plans, and also artifacts of student learning, such as videotapes or audiotapes of student presentations, student writings or drawings, and formal assessment results. The selected artifacts relate to a particular student outcome, which the teacher in an introductory statement identifies. The portfolio also includes a reflective statement in which the teacher analyzes the student learning (indicated by the work in the portfolio), and critiques his or her teaching, specifying modifications inspired by review of the portfolio. Because both teaching and learning are directed to the specific outcome, the portfolio links teaching and learning in a focused way.

Two types of integrated portfolios enable differentiation between novice and experienced teachers. *Comprehensive portfolios* emphasize accountability and provide an in-depth look at novice teachers. *Critical incident portfolios,* while maintaining a level of accountability for experienced teachers, emphasize professional development by respecting their wisdom and providing opportunity for self-evaluation. Critical incident portfolios also reduce the district resources needed to keep a meaningful evaluation system functioning.

Comprehensive Portfolios: Evaluating Novice Teachers
Comprehensive portfolios, the tool for evaluating beginning teachers, state the conceptual goal of a unit, assemble a complete set of evidence about the teaching and learning in the unit, include a detailed narrative of the events that occur in a unit, and diagnose student learning in a reflective statement. Through student outcome statements, descriptions of the unit, and reflective statements, comprehensive portfolios capture teacher thinking in all phases of teaching: planning, teaching, and post-teaching. Comprehensive portfolios link teaching to student learning by including student outcomes in addition to teaching documentation. The teacher speaks to the link between teaching and learning when writing the reflective statement.

> Comprehensive portfolios capture teacher thinking in all phases of teaching: planning, teaching, and post-teaching.

Because comprehensive portfolios include information about all aspects of teaching and learning related to the student outcome, it will be a large document requiring a large amount of time to produce and review. A unit addressing a large concept or fundamental skill will necessarily have occurred over several days or weeks. The evidence will include many video or audiotapes, and the narrative and reflective statements, which require hours to compose.

Rendering informed judgments about the competence of beginning teachers' work based on the information in comprehensive portfolios is the main purpose for their construction. Consequently, a protocol for scoring, including both standards and procedures for review, is essential.

Standards

The standards against which a comprehensive portfolio might be holistically judged are

• *The rationale for selection of the topic.* Do content specialists agree that the topic is significant within the discipline and within relevant broad district or state curriculum guidelines?

• *Articulation of the goals of the unit* (Described in the portfolio). Beyond topic selection, has the specific-learning outcome been clearly stated? Is the relationship between this particular student outcome and the essential concepts of the subject matter indicated?

• *Breadth and creativity of instructional strategies.* Does the teaching include approaches and materials that address a variety of learning styles, chosen for defensible reasons, and that have been adapted specifically for this teaching event?

• *Appropriateness of assessment strategies.* Do the chosen assessment strategies convincingly demonstrate that the students have or have not learned what was intended?

• *Breadth and variety of forms of evidence* (included in the portfolio). Does the portfolio include several forms of evidence: artifacts, productions, reproductions, and attestations (Collins, 1991)? Taken as a set, does the evidence document all aspects of the unit?

• *Quality of the narrative description.* Does the narrative tell a coherent story, linking the elements of the unit together to develop the learning outcome of the unit, and does the narrative present a convincing rationale (including references to underlying beliefs) for the choices and decisions made by the teacher during the unit?

• *Quality of the reflective statement.* Does the statement draw a reasonable conclusion about the depth of student learning of the intended outcome? Is it justified by the student assessment results, and does it include reasonable suggestions for modification when teaching the unit next time?

Portfolio Review

The work of comprehensive portfolio review should be conducted by a team of administrators, subject or grade-level specialists, and experienced teachers using a holistic approach. Team review offers several advantages: objectivity of judgment is improved since decisions involve more than one person; specialist or grade-level expertise is included (important in high schools where no one has deep knowledge in every discipline; important in elementary schools, where all professionals are generalists); and practitioner expertise is included.

> Examination of the evidence is the limiting factor of a review, both because of its quantity and because of the unique nature of many items.

Examination of the evidence is the limiting factor of a review, both because of its quantity and because of the unique nature of many items. (It would be costly and inconvenient to provide a set of tapes for everyone; it could well be impossible to reproduce original student work for everyone). Review of various items might be apportioned to several team members while everyone reads the teachers' goal statement, narrative description, and reflective statement. The teacher might be interviewed about his or her portfolio or asked to summarize it.

The team would convene following each member's review of the evidence. Each would make a brief presentation to the team about preliminary ideas. Following discussion, each member would decide on a rating for the portfolio. Large variations in scores exceeding a predetermined range could be adjudicated by asking members to review the other portions of the evidence or by seeking an additional reviewer. Holding comprehensive portfolio reviews during the summer (current norms about summer notwithstanding) would be optimum for everyone.

Although accountability is the main purpose for the construction of comprehensive portfolios, a professional development component also exists. The act of constructing the portfolio will stimulate deep analysis of teaching by the novice teacher. Critique of the portfolio by a mentor in anticipation of formal review could extend the analysis further. By responding to the questions and comments of a mentor, the novice teacher is preparing for the future when he or she will be expected to present a critical incident portfolio to colleagues. Not insignificantly, the mentor would learn more about teaching and learning as she or he guides a less-experienced colleague in analyzing teaching and learning related to an outcome.

Comprehensive portfolio review becomes the essential step in establishing one's credibility as a competent teacher, and it becomes the ritual that delineates the stages of a teacher's career. At some point, perhaps after three years of successful comprehensive portfolio reviews, the novice teacher has earned the respect and confidence of his or her colleagues. Now the time has come to shift the emphasis in teacher evaluation from accountability to professional development; instead of comprehensive portfolios, the experienced teacher now constructs critical incident portfolios.

> Critical incident portfolios present selected incidents that were particularly provocative and illuminating.

Critical Incident Portfolios

Given the extraordinary resources required to create and review comprehensive portfolios, at a point in experienced teachers' careers, it no longer makes sense to use this method for evaluation. A certain presumption of baseline competence can be made, and a different approach that builds on experienced teachers' competence and makes good use of everyone's time is called for. Use of critical incident portfolios for experienced teachers redefines *evaluation* to mean "an ongoing responsibility to demonstrate one's intellectual activity as a teacher." The main purpose of evaluation for the experienced teacher is now to stimulate deep and meaningful professional development.

Critical incident portfolios have some elements in common with comprehensive portfolios but are more manageable. (See figure 1.) Comprehensive portfolios, as the name implies, are intended to capture every aspect of the teaching of a unit. In contrast, critical incident portfolios present selected incidents that were particularly provocative and illuminating. These incidents are "critical" in that they inspired teacher insight about how to improve the unit next time and about characteristics of one's teaching more generally.

Like comprehensive portfolios, critical incident portfolios include a statement of the rationale for choosing the topic, a clear statement of intended student outcomes, and a reflective

Figure 1
Comparison of Elements in Comprehensive and
Critical Incident Portfolios

Comprehensive Portfolio	Critical Incident Portfolio
* Student Outcome Statement	* Student Outcome Statement
* Brief Description of Unit	* Brief Description of Unit
* Narrative	
* Reflective Statement	* Reflective Statement
* Comprehensive Evidence Set	* Selected Evidence Set

statement. Reflective statements in this type of integrated port-folio name the critical incidents, justify their selection, and indicate the consequent changes in practice. However, critical incident portfolios do not include a narrative statement that explains each element of the unit, and they include only selected bits of evidence that document the critical incidents under discussion. Rather than running hours in length or including dozens of items, the evidence set of a critical incident portfolio includes only minutes of tape and only those artifacts that bear explicitly on the critical incidents under discussion.

Omission of the narrative from the critical incident portfolio and inclusion of only specific bits of evidence are manifestations of the presumed competence of the teacher. We assume that the teacher has defensible reasons for choices made and that the unit if examined as a whole is coherent and includes a broad and creative spectrum of instructional strategies. Critical incident portfolios are intended [to] stimulate critical thinking by the teacher about his or her teaching by creating the portfolio and presenting the portfolio to peers.

Because baseline competence can be assumed for experienced teachers, no formal scoring mechanism is required. In fact, a formal scoring system would inevitably shift the focus away from professional development back to accountability. When doubt arises or persists about the assumption of underlying competence of a particular experienced teacher, comprehensive portfolio review, with its formal scoring rubric, may be required on a case-by-case basis.

Critical incident portfolios can be presented to grade level or content peers during professional development days. The audience will be expected to comment and question in colloquium fashion, stimulating a rich conversation among colleagues that will inspire new ideas for everyone. Professional development originally stimulated by the self-analysis required to construct the critical incident portfolio can be extended in two ways: (1) by requiring the author to participate in conversation with others, and (2) through the connections between the teaching and learning being described for the participants and their own work.

> **Critical incident portfolios can be presented to grade level or content peers during professional development days.**

Colloquia focused on discussion of teaching and learning prompted by the issues contained in a particular portfolio will break down the isolation that now exists among teachers. Such colloquia would provide a forum for dignifying, validating, and developing teachers' professional knowledge. Administrators, supervisors, and perhaps even parents and students would be welcome. The public nature of these colloquia would ensure a level of accountability while simultaneously respecting the wisdom and experience of career teachers. It would create an arena in which the viewpoints of various groups with a stake in education could be constructively expressed.

A system would be devised ensuring that all experienced teachers conducted such colloquia regularly and ensuring whatever level of administrative review as is deemed necessary. Because responsibility for the creation of the portfolio lies with the teacher, the administrator is relieved of the task of annually writing dozens of evaluations. The standards of fine teaching against which the teacher is measuring her- or himself become internalized, and therefore important and legitimate, as opposed to the external standards now imposed on teachers by remote experts whose lack of knowledge about the teacher's class often trivializes those standards in the teacher's eyes.

Some combination of existing practice, where administrators observe in classrooms, and colloquia could be instituted. Relieved of the responsibility of making a judgment, the administrator could watch in the classrooms of experienced teachers with a different eye. Schoolwide conversation about student outcomes fostered by the portfolio presentations and the link between teaching and learning now explicit through the portfolios would inform administrators about the substance of instruction at a level now rarely attained. Relieved of the anxiety and skepticism with which too many teachers now receive visits from administrators, and confident that principals actually know something about the details of instruction, teachers could welcome administrators more openly. Authentic conversation about teaching and learning to which both parties contribute mutually becomes more possible.

Two sample portfolios, one of each type, follow in the balance of this article. They are grounded in the eight weeks I recently spent co-teaching chemistry in an urban high school in a small Connecticut city. Reproduction and space limitations require that only a listing of the evidence sets with captions can be included (unfortunately, videotape cannot be rendered into print). In practice, the goal and reflective statements written by novice and experienced teachers, even when the unit topics are the same, would be very different, but in this case both examples are generated from my experience and so are identical.

GUMDROPS, ATOMS AND CHEMICAL REACTIONS
Student Outcome Statement—Both Comprehensive and Critical Incident Versions
(This portfolio entry identifies the student outcome on which the portfolio focuses and explains the teacher's rationale for selecting it.)

This portfolio documents student understanding of the meaning of chemical symbols and equations, and their understanding that chemical equations symbolically represent changes in physical and chemical properties observable in nature.

Students' understanding will be manifest through (1) their ability to connect concrete models (gumdrops) of reactants and products to the writing and balancing of chemical equations, and (2) their ability to make comparative statements about the chemical and physical properties of reactants and products.

I selected this unit as the topic for my portfolio because the topic is central to chemistry. If students are to achieve the course goal of being able to define chemistry comprehensively, but on their terms, and to express its relationship to their lives, they must understand what a chemical reaction is, and how to interpret symbolic representations of reactions. Using the language of chemistry with ease is not merely useful for students, it is essential to their understanding of the discipline.

Brief Description of the Unit*
(This portfolio entry orients the reader to the topic of the portfolio and indicates how it fits into the overall conceptual structure of the course [secondary] or subject area [elementary]. The asterisk (*) indicates the student outcome that this portfolio focuses on.)

Conceptual Structure of the Course
WHAT IS CHEMISTRY AND HOW DOES IT FIT INTO MY LIFE?
What are chemical reactions?
*What is the meaning conveyed by chemical symbols strung together in chemical equations?

My co-teacher, Robert Johnson, and I each taught separate parts of the unit.* We agreed conceptually what each part should be, what the sequence of the parts should be, and how the parts fit together. We did detailed planning of each of our parts as individuals (with occasional consultation). I began the unit by having students use gumdrops to model events during a chemical reaction. Next Bob demonstrated two chemical reactions and linked the observable changes at the macroscopic level to molecular changes as demonstrated through manipulation of the gumdrops.

The unit ran from October 15 to October 20. The first quiz was administered as a take-home quiz on October 19. Because we were not satisfied with the initial quiz results, reteaching began on October 23 and continued through October 26 when another quiz was administered in class.

Narrative (Comprehensive Version)
(This portfolio entry describes the thinking of the teacher as the unit unfolds.)

A recurring task is to devise interesting and varying ways to cause the students to process textual material. Simply asking students to read sections in the text, even when reinforced by questioning by the teacher in class, is not sufficient to lead students to build deep understanding of the textual material. We designed this unit to assist students with processing the textual material in *CHEMCOM Chemistry in the Community,* Unit One, "The Quality of Our Water," Section B.4, "Molecular View of Water," and B.5 "Symbols and Formulas," pp. 24–26 (American Chemical Society, 1988).

I believe that students must be able to see and touch concrete objects as much as possible to build a solid understanding of a concept. So when faced with the task of teaching students about chemical language as representative of events we can never see, I immediately began searching for models. Bob told me we did have wooden molecular models, which I have used before. In the past I never had quite enough to go around, and I know that when they are dropped, as they inevitably will be, they bounce around, disturbing everybody. So, when another department member told me about using gumdrops to represent atoms, I was immediately interested. I thought they would probably arouse some interest, they would stay in place, and even if dropped, they would not cause a disruptive clatter. Furthermore, they are readily accessible so that I could be sure to have enough for everybody. Last, but not least, I know adolescents love food! I decided to use them.

My next task was to obtain the gumdrops and figure out exactly how to use them. Because we are working in a unit on water, I decided I would begin by having students represent the chemical reaction for the formation of water from hydrogen and oxygen. I expected that I would lead the students through the water example, and then set them to more independent practice representing the reaction for the formation of ammonia. I chose ammonia because it is another common substance, and because the reaction involves coefficients other than one, which require students to think more deeply.

I asked Bob for suggestions about how to distribute the gumdrops, and he came up with the waxed sandwich bags from the cafeteria. A close examination of the candy on shelves at CVS showed me that spearmint was available along with variety bags. I purchased several bags of each type and spent a sticky half-hour counting out toothpicks, six green gumdrops and two not-green gumdrops for each of twelve bags, one bag for each pair of students. Six green gumdrops would represent the six hydrogen atoms in the ammonia reactions; four green would represent the hydrogen atoms in the water reaction. Two not-green would represent two nitrogen atoms in the ammonia example, and two oxygen in the water example.

I go out of my way to avoid teaching science as a foreign language by which I mean the all-too-common practice of writing a technical term on the board with its definition, which students will then memorize but not necessarily understand. However, accurate and appropriate use of technical terms is essential to understanding chemistry, and this topic presented me with many such terms. I decided to address this problem by making a large sheet listing all the terms without their definitions, and then by directing the students to show what the term meant by manipulating their gumdrops. I believed this would teach the terms effectively, painlessly, and with high probability for retention because we would just begin naturally incorporating them into our speech as we worked on the ammonia and water examples.

As my last step in preparation for teaching this topic, I planned general questions that I would ask students, and the actions I would ask them to perform. I did not want to be restricted in movement or flow by having to refer to an actual list so I rehearsed it in my mind. I planned to rely on that preparation and my general content knowledge when teaching. To an uninformed observer, it might appear that I made up the directions as I went along, but actually I enacted a well-rehearsed script (with a few rough spots indicative of the fact that I was performing it for the first time)!

While I was planning this part of the unit, Bob was assembling the materials he needed to demonstrate actual chemical reactions between magnesium and oxygen, and copper and sulfur. We chose these because we were familiar with them, the materials were at hand, they each are somewhat dramatic and arouse interest, their equations are simple and therefore accessible to students at this stage of their learning, and finally the changes in the physical and chemical properties of the reactions and products are easily observable.

The first day, October 15, went essentially as planned. At the end, Bob said he felt that the students understood the water example well but were a little shaky about the ammonia example. I agreed that his conclusions were likely because the ammonia example had been rushed. So on October 16, I planned to ask students to recount the water example for me quickly, and then to lead them through the ammonia example. I expected this to take about 20 minutes after which Bob would perform the reactions.

I was unprepared for the fragile understanding of the water example that the students demonstrated, but I accepted it as a fact to be addressed. The firm understanding which I believed students had constructed didn't exist. Luckily (really by luck only, not by design), I had gumdrops left over. Because they were not counted out for student use, I retaught the lesson, manipulating the gumdrops myself. Bob's reactions were postponed until Monday, October 19.

On Monday, Bob demonstrated the chemical reactions as planned, linking the actual reactions to chemical language by using triangles and circles drawn on the board in place of gumdrops. He distributed the take-home quiz at the end of class. I collected the quizzes on Tuesday, October 20, and then began class by relinking the writing of reactions to Bob's demonstrations. I did this simply as a bridge to a new topic, not with any conscious intent of continuing to build understanding of the old topic. I thought that job was done. Not until I viewed the tapes of the classes on October 19 and 20 did I realize the significance of the omission of closure on October 19, and the still shaky understanding conveyed by Julia's question posed on October 20. Because I did the viewing after I corrected the quizzes, I was surprised and disappointed by the quiz results. In retrospect, I could have at least suspected what they would be.

The goal of this course is to lead students to build their own understanding of chemistry as an intellectual schemata for understanding natural phenomena. This is not possible if they do not understand how chemical language represents what is happening at the molecular level during chemical reactions. So we decided to reteach the topic. On October 21 and 23 (no class on October 22), we went ahead with a planned lab connected to the new topic I had introduced on October 20, and turned to the reteaching (using the quizzes) on October 23. The reteaching was completed on October 26 when the students took another quiz with much-improved results.

Reflective Statement (Comprehensive and Critical Incident Versions)

(This portfolio entry analyzes student learning, linking it to teaching. The entry also describes the teacher's ideas for changes in the next iteration of the unit as they emerge from his or her analysis of the unit.)

As I analyze the student understanding constructed during this unit, I am satisfied that we achieved our goal. Almost every student achieved an acceptable level of success in moving back and forth between the concrete representations of chemical equations and the symbolic representations of chemical equations. Additionally, I also see changes I would make next time.

The quiz questions specifically require students to link concrete models, which they draw, to written chemical equations, and they require students to compare the chemical and physical properties of reactants and products. Fifteen of twenty-three students scored 80 or better on the second quiz, and only two students scored below 70. These results are acceptable to me. They cluster results at the high end—always a goal of mine. Of the two students who scored below 70, one of them did much better on the initial quiz, leading me to suspect that his low score this time might be idiosyncratic. One student has not constructed the necessary understanding at all, a fact that is simultaneously reasonable (only one student is in this state) and unacceptable (I will not give up on anyone). I regret that I did not analyze the results at this level soon enough to respond to her, and I must make a special point of tracking her understanding from this point.

The fact that Julia asked a pivotal question revealing lack of understanding of the distinction between the terms *atom* and *molecule* on October 20, the day the students handed in their first quiz, is troubling. Julia is one of the strongest students in the class. If she didn't get such an important point, I know others didn't either, a fact which was borne out by the first quiz results. My observation in my journal, p. 48–52, where I lament that Bob did not close adequately before administering the quiz, takes on added significance in light of Julia's question the following day. Perhaps if he had asked the students to reveal the state of their construction of understanding, as I did after the quiz review on October 26 (although only because Tyrone pushed me into it), perhaps we would have caught their incomplete understanding and decided to delay the assessment until we addressed it. I must continuously remind myself of the significance of closure, which I now define as an activity or set of questions that cause students to reveal the state of their understanding. The results of closure indicate whether the time for assessment has arrived or not. Omission of closure can lead to premature assessment, which is what happened to us here.

The content of Julia's question leads me to three refinements of this unit for the next time. First, I must do a more thorough job of eliciting what students know about the vocabulary of the unit before moving into manipulating the models to represent the changes occurring during chemical reactions. The October 15 tape indicates a superficial swipe at this, but a more extensive series of questions that ask the students to use the models to represent atoms, molecules, compounds, and elements would lay a firmer foundation for the more complicated manipulations required to represent chemical reactions.

The second refinement would be embedded in the first. I noticed that student's themselves began to use the language of sets to distinguish between atoms and molecules. I should build on that transfer of learning quite deliberately by using set language myself from the outset. For example, I could say an atom is a set containing one and only one particle, and a molecule is a set containing at least two particles. If the particles in a molecule are identical, the substance is an element. If the particles are different, the substance is a compound. (A question that would test students' understanding of the consequences of this is, Do compounds ever occur in nature as atoms, and how do you know?) Use of this approach might head off Julia's confusion about why Bob used the term *atoms* for magnesium even when reading coefficients from an equation.

Overall, I believe we underestimated the level of difficulty of this concept. I assumed on October 16 that students would easily recount for me the construction of water molecules based on what they had learned on October 15, but five minutes into the class I realized that we essentially needed to repeat the activities of the day before. As the third refinement to the unit, I would elaborate the use of gumdrops in several ways. First, I would plan on having gumdrops available for two days at least, allotting more time for students to construct understanding by actually handling the models. Second, I would have enough gumdrops for *each* student. Finally, I would ask the students to use gumdrops themselves to represent the actual chemical reactions that we demonstrate for them in addition to using circles and triangles on the board. At this point, I could ask some students to represent the first reaction; others the second. Each student could then demonstrate his or her reaction to a student who had represented the other one. Also at this stage I could ask students to select their own colors, and figure out for themselves how many of each color they need. (I will need a much larger supply of gumdrops!)

Finally, analysis of this unit leads me to believe we missed an opportunity to support student development of an even bigger idea in chemistry than the one on which this portfolio focuses. Although I linked the rearrangement of atoms into different molecules as represented by our gumdrops to the two actual reactions Bob did, we didn't assess student understanding of this concept. We should. This is an aspect of what I would want to see at the course's conclusion when I ask students to define chemistry in their own terms, so we should take advantage of recurring opportunities to develop deeper and deeper understanding of this concept.

Listing of Evidence with Captions (Comprehensive Version)
(This entry describes each piece of evidence included in the portfolio. Arranged chronologically, the items in the set draw a comprehensive picture of the teacher's mental and physical activity as well as students' learning.)

1. *Journal entries, pp. 10a-2, 11a-2.* These two entries are my initial plan for teaching the unit.

2. *Sheet listing technical terms.* This is the list of technical terms that I expected students to understand as a result of manipulating the gumdrops.

3. *Video tape, 10/15/92, and journal entry, p. 18-2.* The tape records the initial teaching of chemical symbolism and equations, and the entry records my initial analysis of it.

4. *Journal entry, p. 22a-2.* This entry records my plan for continuation of teaching the unit.

5. *Videotape, 10/16/92, and journal entry, p. 25-2.* The tape records the second day of teaching chemical symbolism and equations, and the entry is my analysis of the teaching.

6. *Videotape, 10/19/92, and journal entries, p. 27-2, and p. 48-2.* The tape records Bob teaching about the relationship between the written chemical equations and actual chemical reactions. The first entry is my analysis of his teaching; the second entry records insights I had while watching the tape several days later.

7. *Quiz results, 10/20/92, and journal entry, p. 31-2.* The entry expresses my ambivalence about the results: on the whole, the set was better than work we had received earlier on other topics but not good enough to convince me that the students have accurately constructed the understanding we seek. The entry also indicates my plan for reteaching.

8. *First half of videotape, 10/20/92.* I synthesize the microscopic and macroscopic aspects of the unit. Julia's question reveals incomplete construction of understanding (and this is after our first assessment).

9. *Audiotape, 10/26/92, second-quiz results, 10/26/92, and journal entry, p. 35-2.* Audiotape records student expression of imperfect construction of understanding and how, as an entire group, we all help each other adjust. Quiz results indicate improved understanding over the first quiz, and the entry documents my response.

Listing of Evidence with Captions (Critical Incident Version)
(This entry identifies the selected pieces of evidence documenting the critical incidents discussed in the reflective statement.
Here the items are arranged to correspond to the order of discussion of the incidents in the reflective statement.)

 1. *Segment from videotape of October 20: Julia's Question.*
This segment shows Julia asking about the difference between
atoms and molecules as prompted by the phrase *2 Mg*. She
wants to know why Bob read this phrase as "two magnesium
atoms" instead of "two magnesium molecules."

 2. *Journal entry, p. 48-2 to 50-2: Reactions to viewing tape
of October 19.* This entry recounts my emerging understanding
of the difficulty of the chemical symbol system for students, my
first notion that using set language might be helpful, and my
observation that the lack of closure to the demonstration of
chemical reactions was critical.

 3. *Segment from October 19 tape: Demonstration of Chemical Reactions.* This segment shows Bob finishing the discussion
of reactions and distributing the quiz without closure.

 4. *Take-home quiz results.* Here I show a frequency distribution of the results and include several papers indicating representative errors. Examination of a paper indicates that the
questions asked do assess the goal of the unit.

 5. *Segment from October 26 audiotape: Tyrone Forces Closure.* This segment shows how Tyrone's lack of confidence in
himself pushes me to close the reteaching by posing an example
to the class, which they solve perfectly.

 6. *Second quiz results.* Here I show a frequency distribution again and include Susan's perfect paper to illustrate the
questions asked. I chose Susan's paper because she had been
convinced that she should drop the course despite her goal of
becoming a nurse. How wonderful that she was wrong!

CONCLUSION

In 1988, Costa, Garmston, and Lambert alerted educators to
one of the great myths of our profession: that teacher-evaluation practices have improved instruction for students. No lack
of will exists on the part of teachers, administrators, or those
designing teacher-evaluation systems toward this end. Yet, in
his 1986 study, Glickman was unable to find any evidence supporting this notion.

The integrated portfolio model for teacher evaluation proposes an innovative approach to teacher development and evaluation, and holds promise for more direct and meaningful outcomes for both teachers and students. Perhaps the most important result of the proposed model is that which is gained by the teachers themselves, as they engage in inquiry about their own teaching and move into the role of researcher. Rather than being passive recipients of another's inspection and appraisal, teachers begin to observe themselves and their students carefully, to analyze critically the results of particular teaching episodes, and to make determinations about the effectiveness of their teaching as evidenced in the learning of their students. The model presents a stimulating professional exercise whereby teachers sharpen skills of thinking about and judging their own performance, become more self-directed, and refine their abilities to modify their own work toward the end of student success at attaining important and meaningful learning outcomes.

> The integrated portfolio model for teacher evaluation proposes an innovative approach to teacher development and evaluation.

Although the main purpose of teacher evaluation differs for novice and experienced teachers, nonetheless this outcome of the use of integrated portfolios for teacher evaluation pertains to both groups. While constructing comprehensive portfolios, especially with the guidance of a mentor, novice teachers are developing the critical eye they will need for their future construction of critical incident portfolios. Conversely, experienced teachers serving as either portfolio reviewers or mentors are constructing deep understanding about standards for excellent teaching, which they will bring to bear when constructing their critical incident portfolios and as they conduct colloquia about their portfolios.

When constructed as outlined in this proposal, integrated portfolios offer several advantages over traditional teacher evaluation processes:

1. They generate information about the cognitive aspects of teaching.
2. They explicitly connect teaching to student outcomes.

3. They offer differentiated evaluation processes for novice and experienced teachers.

4. They stimulate rich, intellectual conversations among teachers, and between teachers and administrators.

5. They assume accountability as an accepted professional norm.

6. They function without inordinate demands on administrator time.

7. They lead teachers to internalize standards for excellence in teaching related directly to student learning.

8. They shift responsibility for documenting proficiency from the administrator to the teacher.

The integrated portfolios illustrated here are the beginning of a new discussion about the ways in which schools are run. They prompt questions about the appropriateness of certain aspects of current school structure and certain current norms of practice for both teachers and administrators. Under the auspices of the Professional Educator Development Program (PED) sponsored by the Connecticut State Department of Education, investigation of their promise for improving teaching and learning will continue.

NOTES

1. The author expresses her thanks to Marjorie Anctil for her invaluable comments about earlier drafts of this article.
2. The work described in this article was funded in part by the Connecticut State Department of Education, in part by the National Science Foundation through a Systemic School Initiative Grant awarded to the Connecticut State Department of Education, and in part by a Small Grant from the Spencer Foundation.

REFERENCES

Anctil, M. (1990). *Distinguishing between behaviors and decision making origins of beginning, exprienced and expert teachers.* Unpublished dissertation. Bridgeport, CT: University of Bridgeport.

American Chemical Society. (1988). *CHEMCOM chemistry in the community.* Dubuque, IA: Kendall/Hunt Publishing Company.

Berliner, D. (1986). In pursuit of the expert pedagogue. *Educational Researcher,* (15), 5–13.

Bird, T. (1990). The schoolteacher portfolio: an essay on possibilities. In Millman, J., and Darling-Hammond, L. (Eds.), *The new handbook of teacher evaluation: assessing elementary and secondary school teachers.* Newbury Park, CA: Sage Publications.

Collins, A. (1991). Portfolios for biology teacher assessment. In *Journal of Personnel Evaluation in Education.* Kluwer Academic Publishers, (5), 147–167.

Costa, A. L., Garmston, R. J., and Lambert, L. (1988). Evaluation of teaching: the cognitive development view. In Stanley, Sarah J., and Popham, W. James. (Eds.), *Teacher evaluation: six prescriptions for success.* Alexandria, VA: The Association for Supervision and Curriculum Development.

Glickman, C. (1986). *Supervision for increasing teacher thought and commitment.* Paper presented at the National Curriculum Study Institute. New Orleans.

Millman, J., and Darling-Hammond, L. (Eds.) (1990). *The new handbook of teacher evaluation: assessing elementary and secondary school teachers.* Newbury Park, CA: Sage Publications.

Regan, H. B., Anctil, M., Dubea, C., Hofmann, J. M., and Vaillancourt, R. (1992). *Teacher: a new definition and model for development and evaluation.* Philadelphia: RBS Publications.

Schwab, R. L. (Ed.) (1990). *Research-based teacher evaluation: a special issue of the journal of personnel evaluation in education.* Boston: Kluwer Academic Publishers.

Wolf, Kenneth. (1991). The schoolteacher's portfolio: issues in design, implementation, and evaluation. *Phi Delta Kappan,* 73(7), 129–136.

Authors

Navaz Peshotan Bhavnagri is an associate professor in early childhood education at Wayne State University, Detroit. She teaches a course involving portfolios for young children and has written on her work in this area.

Don M. Boileau, professor and chair of the Communication Department, co-directs the portfolio instructional program at George Mason University.

James Boyer is assistant dean for Academic Services at Wayne State University, Detroit. He has served as director of student teaching and has taught extensively in the area of secondary education.

Lucindia H. Chance is assistant dean and professor at the University of Memphis, where she was instrumental in implementing the Professional Development School concept in eleven partner schools.

Mary E. Dietz, an international consultant, works with educational systems in systemic change and facilitating learning communities using a constructivist approach to learning and leading. She co-authored *Who Will Save Our Schools: Teachers as Constructivist Leaders.*

Mary E. Diez is professor of education and dean of the School of Education at Alverno College, Milwaukee. A 1995 winner of the McGraw Education prize, she has worked extensively in performance assessment design at Alverno.

Sharon Elliott, whose area of expertise is early childhood education, is assistant dean of teacher education at Wayne State University in Detroit. She is a principal investigator of a number of grant projects, including an alternative pathways to teaching project, funded by the Dewitt-Wallace Foundation.

Jeffrey I. Gelfer is an associate professor of early childhood education at the University of Nevada, Las Vegas.

Estelle S. Gellman is a professor in the educational research program at Hofstra University in Hempstead, New York. She is the author of *School Testing: What Parents and Educators Need to Know.*

Christine Hult is a professor and assistant department head in the English Department at Utah State University in Logan, Utah. Recent publications include *Evaluating Teachers of Writing* and *Researching & Writing Across the Curriculum.*

Peggy G. Perkins is an associate professor of educational psychology at the University of Nevada, Las Vegas.

Thomas A. Rakes is professor and dean of the College of Education at Northeast Louisiana University. He has authored and co-authored more than eighty refereed articles and book chapters, as well as nine college textbooks.

Helen B. Regan is professor of education at Connecticut College in New London and is a former high school chemistry teacher and principal. She is co-author of *Out of Women's Experience: Creating Relational Leadership.*

Jo-Ann Snyder is director of field experiences at Wayne State University in Detroit. Formerly a teacher and an administrator with the Detroit Public Schools, she continues to be interested in the preparation of effective urban teachers.

Patricia H. Wheeler, president of EREAPA Associates in Livermore, California, has written extensively on assessment and teacher evaluation. She has consulted with the federally-funded Center for Research on Educational Accountability and Teacher Evaluation (CREATE) at Western Michigan University.

Kenneth Wolf, formerly a research assistant with the Teacher Assessment Project at Stanford University, is an assistant professor in the School of Education at the University of Colorado at Denver. He has worked with teacher portfolios in schools and districts, for the Texas and Colorado state departments of education, and at the National Board for Professional Teaching Standards.

Acknowledgments

Grateful acknowledgment is made to the following authors and agents for their permission to reprint copyrighted materials.

SECTION 1

The Association of Teacher Educators for "Beyond Assessment: University/School Collaboration in Portfolio Review and the Challenge to Program Improvement" by Jo-Ann Snyder, Sharon Elliott, Navaz Peshotan Bhavnagri, and James Boyer. From *Action in Teacher Education,* vol. 15, no. 4, pp. 55–60, Winter 1993–1994. Copyright © 1993 by the Association of Teacher Educators. Reprinted with permission. All rights reserved.

Mary E. Diez for "The Portfolio: Sonnet, Mirror and Map" by Mary E. Diez. A paper presented at the Conference on Linking Liberal Arts and Teacher Education: Encouraging Reflection through Portfolios (San Diego, California, October 6, 1994). Copyright © 1994 by Mary E. Diez. Reprinted with permission. All rights reserved.

Lucindia H. Chance and Thomas A. Rakes for "Differentiated Evaluation in Professional Development Schools: An Alternative Paradigm for Preservice Teacher Evaluation" by Lucindia H. Chance and Thomas A. Rakes. A paper presented at the CREATE National Evaluation Institute (Gatlinburg, Tennessee, July 10–15, 1994). Copyright © 1994 by Lucindia H. Chance and Thomas A. Rakes. Reprinted with permission. All rights reserved.

SECTION 2

The Association for Supervision and Curriculum Development (ASCD) for "Developing an Effective Teaching Portfolio" by Kenneth Wolf. From *Educational Leadership,* pp. 34–37, March 1996. Copyright © 1996 by ASCD. Reprinted with permission. All rights reserved.

SECTION 3

Kluwer Academic Publishers—Boston for "Integrated Portfolios as Tools for Differentiated Teacher Education: A Proposal" by Helen B. Regan. From *Journal of Personnel Evaluation in Education,* vol. 7, no. 4, pp. 275–290, December 1993. Copyright © 1993 by Kluwer Academic Publishers—Boston. Reprinted with permission. All rights reserved.

Index

Learn from Our Books *and* from Our Authors!

Bring Our Author/Trainers to Your District

At IRI/SkyLight, we have assembled a unique team of outstanding author/trainers with international reputations for quality work. Each has designed high-impact programs that translate powerful new research into successful learning strategies for every student. We design each program to fit your school's or district's special needs.

Training Programs

IRI/SkyLight's training programs extend the renewal process by helping educators move from content-centered to mind-centered classrooms. In our highly interactive workshops, participants learn foundational, research-based information and teaching strategies in an instructional area that they can immediately transfer to the classroom setting. With IRI/SkyLight's specially prepared materials, participants learn how to teach their students to learn for a lifetime.

Network for Systemic Change

Through a partnership with Phi Delta Kappa, IRI/SkyLight offers a Network for site-based systemic change: *The Network of Mindful Schools.* The Network is designed to promote systemic school change as possible and practical when starting with a renewed vision that centers on *what* and *how* each student learns. To help accomplish this goal, Network consultants work with member schools to develop an annual tactical plan and then implement that plan at the classroom level.

Training of Trainers

The Training of Trainers programs train your best teachers, those who provide the highest quality instruction, to coach other teachers. This not only increases the number of teachers you can afford to train in each program, but also increases the amount of coaching and follow-up that each teacher can receive from a resident expert. Our Training of Trainers programs will help you make a systemic improvement in your staff development program.

To receive a FREE COPY of the IRI/SkyLight catalog or more information about trainings offered through IRI/SkyLight, contact CLIENT SERVICES at

TRAINING AND PUBLISHING, INC.
2626 S. Clearbrook Dr., Arlington Heights, IL 60005
800-348-4474 • 847-290-6600 • FAX 847-290-6609

There are
one-story intellects,
two-story intellects, and three-story
intellects with skylights. All fact collectors, who
have no aim beyond their facts, are one-story men. Two-story men
compare, reason, generalize, using the labors of the fact collectors as
well as their own. Three-story men idealize, imagine,
predict—their best illumination comes from
above, through the skylight.

—*Oliver Wendell*

Holmes

TRAINING AND PUBLISHING, INC.